THE GREAT
INTERIOR DESIGN
CHALLENGE
SOURCEBOOK

THE GREAT INTERIOR DESIGN CHALLENGE SOURCEBOOK

PAVILION

THE GREAT INTERIOR DESIGN CHALLENGE

In the new series of *The Great Interior Design Challenge*, 27 talented amateur designers competed over 16 episodes, for a chance to win the coveted title.

Presenter and architectural historian Tom Dyckhoff oversaw proceedings, while judges – President of the British Institute of Interior Design, Daniel Hopwood and interior stylist and magazine journalist Sophie Robinson – decided who had the vision and the skill to be the next big thing in design.

In this series the competitors travelled the length and breadth of the country, and also though the ages – from medieval homes to contemporary eco blocks. To ensure a level playing field in each qualifying round, three would-be interior designers took on similar rooms in three neighbouring properties. They had three days, £1,000 and the help of a small team to interpret homeowners' briefs and bring their designs to fruition.

The amateur designers came from all walks of life, and included a librarian, a college lecturer, a civil servant and a restaurant manager. All believed they had the skills and creativity required to make it in the world of interior design. But as the designers moved further along in the competition, the briefs and the rooms became increasingly challenging – and the judges' expectations were higher than ever.

In the nine heats the amateurs redesigned rooms in a huge array of buildings: 17th-century cottages in the Cotswolds; 1920s beach huts in Poole; crooked bedrooms in medieval homes; terraced houses in the heart of London's East End; colourful fishermen's cottages in Brixham, Devon; neo-Georgian houses in Welwyn Garden City; 21st-century eco homes in Greater London; Dutch-influenced cottages in Port Sunlight, Wales; and 1930s apartments built for the film stars of the day.

The nine heat winners then went through to the second round, where some transformed bedrooms in Kentish oast houses, others worked on front rooms in handsome Edwardian homes in Wimbledon, while the final group designed reception rooms on houseboats on the River Thames.

In the two quarter-final programmes, the designers faced their trickiest rooms yet – one group in double-height rooms in an Edwardian school conversion in London, and the other in a 1960s complex in Surrey.

The two winners from each of the quarter finals went through to the semi-final, where they all travelled to Scotland to design rooms in Edinburgh's famous tenements. This time they had a bigger budget of £1,500, so the judge's expectations were even higher.

For the final the two best amateurs battled it out in an elegant stately home in Cumbria. They had £4,000 and three rooms to transform in just four days. It was their toughest challenge yet, but one talented designer overcame the final hurdle to be crowned the champion of *The Great Interior Design Challenge*.

Tom Dyckhoff

'Architecture and design doesn't have to be unapproachable – interior design is something that we can all do to connect to our homes and reflect our character.'

Tom has written widely for publications from *The Sunday Telegraph* to *GQ* and has written a weekly column for *The Guardian*'s 'Weekend' magazine for more than a decade. He was also architecture critic for *The Times* from 2003 to 2011.

He is the architecture critic for the BBC's weekly arts programme, *The Culture Show*, and has written and presented many documentaries on British television and radio – including *The Secret Life of Buildings* on Channel 4, *Saving Britain's Past* on BBC2 and *Room With A View* on Radio 4.

Tom is currently writing his first book – on architecture and cities since the 1970s.

Daniel Hopwood

'You can't learn about interior design, it has to be in your soul as a passion – passion that comes from going around stately homes at the age of six and loving it, or nicking your sister's dolls house and re-jigging its spatial planning.'

Trained as an architect, Daniel set up his own interior design company in '93 which from humble beginnings is now one of the most renowned design studios in London, so much so that his fellow interior designers have appointed him as President of their professional body the British Institute of Interior Design.

Occasionally he dips into the world of television, the last time ten years ago as the judge on Channel 4's *Britain's Best Homes*, and again now as the judge for BBC2's *The Great Interior Design Challenge*.

Sophie Robinson

'You don't have to go into posh houses to see beautiful interiors; you can find them in the most unexpected homes in Britain.'

Sophie Robinson has been in the interior design business for almost 20 years, earning the reputation as one of the industry's top interior stylists. After studying furniture design at university, Sophie went on to produce her own range of lighting for Liberty. She then moved into journalism, becoming Home Editor for BBC *GoodHomes* magazine.

Since setting up her own business she has continued to write for a number of interiors magazines such as *Ideal Home*, *House Beautiful* and *Homes and Gardens*. She has also appeared on BBC, ITV and Channel 5.

SERIES 1 CONTESTANTS

JANE BEALE

'I have been told I have a talent for creating a luxurious, polished but homely look.' Mum and part-time events co-ordinator Jane from Kent, likes to use colour, texture and accessories to create living spaces that are inviting and stylish as well as functional.

HELEN BOTTRILL

'If I can't find what I want, I make it, it's easy.' Helen lives in Devon and designs and creates bespoke textiles from her collection of bold fabrics. Her style is a mismatching mix of the old and the new and she believes that everyone's home should reflect their personality.

DEE CARTWRIGHT

'Interiors is not what I do anymore ... it's who I am now.' Dee is a housewife from Kent who believes that interior design should make someone feel that their space is utterly personal to them. Her style is New England meets English country.

ANNA CHAPMAN

'I'm like David Bowie; I don't stick to one era or style.' A retired optician from London, Anna believes she has always had an interest in interiors. Her style is always evolving and she likes to have the flexibility to change a room every few years.

HELEN CHARLTON

'Your home has to feel relaxed with treasures around you, each with their own story.' Helen is a part-time teacher from Durham who also runs her own craft business. Her French farmhouse-style home has featured in several publications including Country Homes & Interiors.

JOHNNY CHINA

'What I love about interior design is creating something that has personality.' Currently based in Devon, painter and decorator Johnny is interested in all aspects of design and has a retro eclectic style. He is now retraining and hopes to pursue a career in interiors.

JORDAN CLUROE

'I'd absolutely love to be an interior designer ... I think I'd be quite good.' A coffee-shop owner from London, Jordan has renovated several properties and loves all aspects of interior design. He believes in good design, but thinks functionality is just as important.

ALICE DAVIES

'I love the transformative feeling of well-being a really beautifully designed space can offer and all the compliments I receive when I have visitors!' Full-time mum Alice from East Sussex has an adventurous spirit when it comes to design, and likes using strong colours.

JENNY ELESMORE

'A nice home is one where you sit down and say "ahhh".' Jenny owns a lifestyle shop in Cornwall. She believes homes don't have to be over complicated by style and you can achieve a great look with a little imagination. Her style istraditional with a modern twist.

SUSAN GARRETT

'I don't like to follow trends; I like to be unique.' With five children and four grandchildren, Susan from Kent has dedicated her life to her family, but has always enjoyed designing her home. Her style is colourful and she likes interesting rooms in which people can discover things.

NEIL GAUKWIN

'I do get an enjoyable feeling from looking at a space that I've created.' Neil from East Sussex loves experimenting with second-hand items: his style is 'updated granny chic'. A creative by trade, he likes to take ordinary objects and reuse them in new ways.

JAMES GOSTELOW

'I'm very English and thrive off British designers.' An asset manager from Surrey, James says he lives and breathes interiors and never fully switches off. His style is ultimately traditional with a modern edge and he believes it is integral to be true to the property's period.

PAULA HOLLAND

'I love taking an unloved, neglected space and making it liveable again.' Paula is a pub landlady in Herefordshire and has renovated a number of properties including her pub, which has two Bed & Breakfast rooms. Her style is homely and comfortable.

LYNNE LAMBOURNE

'It started aged seven … when I was re-arranging my bedroom.' Based in Buckinghamshire, Lynne runs her own children's fashion business. Her style is 'Scandi-chic' and she believes that everyone can make their home feel different with a little time and effort.

JULIA MATTHEWS

'I have a great eye for detail and can capture the qualities of a room.' A commercialisation co-ordinator from Nottingham, Julia also runs her own business that creates artwork out of children's handprints. She describes her style is minimalist but homely.

EMMA MCDONALD

'I make vintage doll's houses to stop me changing my own!' A self-employed vintage homeware and craft dealer from Manchester, Emma has her own blog and has designed 11 homes according to her evolving style, which is currently modern retro chic.

SARAH MOORE

'I buy second hand and old furniture and give it a new lease of life.' Sarah from West Sussex trained as a chef and worked in catering before starting an online vintage shop and writing about vintage style. She favours a colourful and eclectic vintage look.

KIMBERLY PLESTED

'I hate clichés but interior design is my life.' A mum and student from Oxfordshire, Kimberly is now pursuing her childhood dream of studying interior design. With a simple and natural style she loves bringing unique ideas to life.

LOUISE RUMMERY

'I am unable to walk into someone's house and not check out what they have (or usually haven't) done to the space.' An executive assistant from Hampshire, Louise describes her style as bold and dramatic, masculine but with a feminine touch.

LORNA SATCHELL

'Interior design is about not being afraid and saying, "Actually I like this and this is how I want to display it".' Lorna from Birmingham is passionate about blending modern and traditional styles and prides herself on being frugal and thrifty.

AMY TOLLAFIELD

'I don't want to chase trends; I have my own spin on things.' Born in Cornwall but now based in Somerset, freelance artist Amy also runs a small business selling items she makes out of driftwood.
Her design style is bohemian and coastal.

NIGEL TOOZE

'I've always been obsessed with interiors – now I'm taking a giant leap and want to make a career out of it.' Nigel from London is taking time off from his work as a financial lawyer to explore the possibility of working as an interior designer. His style is classical theatrical.

LUKE WATKINS

'My talent lies in being able to understand someone else's taste quickly.' A sales assistant in Oxfordshire, Luke studied interior and spatial design and has worked in the building trade. He describes his style as 'rustic meets modern', and likes skip and loft rummage finds.

CHARMAINE WHITE

'I eat sleep and breathe everything interior design.' A design student from London, with a background in retail Charmaine believes interior designing is about taking people outside of their comfort zones. Her style is sophisticated, chic and modern.

SERIES 2 CONTESTANTS

JO ABRAM

As a child Jo's parents renovated properties and that ignited her passion for interiors. With a talent for seeing the potential in items she finds at car boot sales, Johanna is in her element when she has a project to complete. She's passionate about all things retro and vintage.

MEHUL ASHRA

Born and bred in London, Mehul grew up in a liberal, artistic household. He redesigned his family house to create a 'clean, elegant, beautiful home with a contemporary injection of Hindu iconography.' He has a thoughtful approach, and likes to transform rooms into 'serene spaces of art and solace.'

FRANCESCA BARTON

'A home should reflect the people who live in it, not what's in vogue.' Mum of four Francesca uses her Finnish heritage to inspire her designs. Genuinely and authentically 'shabby chic', with a love of upcycling, she learned her style from her mother who was always changing the family home.

HONOR BATES

'I love functional beauty and practicality.' Born and raised in rural Australia, by a mother who inspired a love of nature and passed along her skill for making the most of what is available, part-time nanny Honor has decided to pursue her dream to become an interior designer.

CHRISTINE BOYLE

Alongside a variety of creative jobs, Christine has spent the last eight years renovating and decorating her home in Belfast, which is her pride and joy. The only new items she has bought are the bed, dining room table and sofa, everything else she has found, made or upcycled.

ALEX BRUCE

Having studied Fashion Design at the London College of Fashion Alex became fascinated with mid-century modern design. He collects furniture and accessories from the period, and his passion for design has helped him to gain a vast knowledge for products and styles that work together.

RICH CARR

Rich is slowly transforming his 400-year-old cottage in Somerset into the perfect home for his family. A furniture upholstery evening class inspired a love of interiors and now they are all he can think about – he is itching to open his own interior design practice.

JANE COLLINS

'I like to bring the birds and flowers into the house ... interior design is just in me.' Busy mum and step-mum, Jane has moved house 13 times over the years. She believes a room should make you feel relaxed and comfortable and enjoys transforming tired objects into gorgeous pieces.

LEILA FORTESCUE

'The excitement of having a white box, and being able to change it ... is what I love.' With a background in design and a love of all things creative, Leila loved decorating her flat for herself and her family. She enjoys working with bold shapes and images, particularly in monochrome.

HANNAH GEE

'I'd describe my style as colourful. There's colour everywhere.' Hannah runs an online business selling items for the home that she finds at antique fairs and car boot sales. She is forever rearranging her house and takes inspiration from everything and everyone that crosses her path.

LACEY HENRY-STEAD

'I live and breathe interior design – I look everywhere for inspiration.' As well as working as a librarian, Lacey has completed two interior design courses. She keeps an eye on the latest trends while drawing inspiration from the past. Her big dream is to 'breathe new, colourful life into British homes.'

JACK HOE

Restaurant manager Jack describes his design talent as raw and untapped. He has filled his house with bargain finds and likes to leave them in their natural state. His friends always ask for his creative advice and he would love to make a career out of interior design.

MARTIN HOLLAND

'I love people coming into my home and being taken aback by it.' A civil servant from Nottingham, Martin loves the transformational aspect of designing and seeing his ideas come to life, and likes to combine structural and spatial changes with the softer side of interiors.

SANDY KELLY

Sandy from Liverpool first became interested in interiors at a young age and later began restoring and selling antiques from her home. With a flair for creating interiors much admired by friends and family, she loves nothing more than finding items to upcycle.

BECKY LINDON

'I like minimalist style and design, with a bit of a quirky twist ...' With a background in video game marketing, Becky is determined to make a career out of her love of design and has recently completed a diploma at the National Design Academy. Becky is passionate about colour but uses it carefully.

KATE MACEY

'My signature style is country, warm, relaxed ...' Teashop owner Kate from Somerset has always been interested in interiors and has a passion for all things vintage. She favours a smart, country look with a few specially picked rustic pieces of furniture, and is also a fan of quirky fabrics.

SCOTT NORVAL

'This is more than just a hobby ... I live for interior design.' As an architectural/structural draughtsman, Scott has always had an eye for detail, but also has a passion for design. He likes to find a balance between minimalism, comfort and practicality, putting his edgy spin on it.

LUCY PASS

'I love making things from scratch and making rooms beautiful.' Based in Lancaster, Lucy runs her own company, designing and making clothes and jewellery. She wants to move into designing interiors so that she can bring all aspects of her love of design together.

CHARLOTTE PEARSON

'The words sumptuous, luxurious and thoughtful sum up my style.' Originally from Yorkshire, Charlotte now lives in Kent with her husband and two little girls. In 2010 they moved into their dream home that dates back to the 1480s and the renovation has been a true labour of love.

SCOTT ROGERS

'I confess: I've got feminine style.' After working in the fashion industry, Scott started his furniture company in 2011. Spontaneous and pro-active, he is confident when it comes to colour and loves mixing his own shades of paint – to use on his furniture and also for the walls of his home.

KELLY SPARKES

Originally from Lancashire, Kelly now lives Hertfordshire and has undertaken a few major renovation projects in her time. She seeks out interesting home accessories, something she has turned into a business, and strives to put her own 'glamorous' stamp on every room she touches.

MICHAEL VAUGHAN

'Change a room and you change the people that enter and leave it ...' An actor based in London, Michael has a passion for furniture and finding bargains. He always wants to give others advice about their interiors, but has learnt to internalise his inner designer!

ANNE WAKEFIELD

'I get excited by an empty room!' A teacher with a background in product design, Anne loves to make her classroom aesthetically inspiring and is known for making a massive effort with her artistic displays. Outside the classroom, Anne fulfils her creative urges by learning new crafts.

EGON WALESCH

'What I love about interior design is its ability to make people happy.' Following encouragement from friends and neighbours, Egon has recently swapped a career as a Programme Manager for one in interior design. He does all his own painting and decorating and loves restoring and upcycling furniture.

LUKE WELLS

'I love being able to see current design trends and interpret and recreate them for myself and others.' Based in Manchester, freelance stylist Luke loves interiors and upcycling furniture. He enjoys finding ways to make ordinary objects and blank wall spaces look more creative and interesting.

LOUISE WILKINSON

Louise bought her first house aged 19 and has had a penchant for doing up cottages ever since. Following a career in hairdressing, she now runs her own online business painting and upcycling furniture. Louise has a strong recycle and reuse ethic and enjoys using eco-friendly products in her creations.

FIONA WILSON

A lecturer and mother to four grown-up boys, Fiona has a history of buying old dilapidated houses, doing them up and then selling them. Her current home is a six-bedroom Victorian manor house in Plymouth, and she has devoted hours to designing every room.

CONTENTS

GOING ROOM BY ROOM 116

WORKING FROM THE OUTSIDE IN

THE EXTERIOR

Whatever type of property you live in, the way it looks from the outside is very important. Just as the way you design your home says as much about you as the clothes you wear, so too does the way you treat the exterior.

While a house should obviously appeal to its owner or occupier, it should also fit in with its surroundings – the road it's in, the buildings or houses next door, or even the countryside around it. Today, we are much more aware of protecting our architectural heritage, hence we have listed buildings and conservation areas. In both cases, the treatment of exteriors is to varying degrees stipulated – there are limitations on what you can and cannot do.

If you live in an individual, detached property then you can treat your home on its own merits, but if you live in a terrace then it will be in everyone's interest to take account of neighbours' properties. Maybe paint your house in a colour that complements the houses on either side, or even get together with your neighbours to decorate the outsides. When it comes to aesthetics, it is a good idea to be true to the essential character of the house, or at least to the one that it is trying to assume.

It's all very well to look stylish and attractive, but on a functional level, the exterior must provide an efficient and serviceable shell for the interior. Exteriors – façades, roofs, woodwork, gates and fences – should be well-maintained so that they are totally weatherproof and resilient.

When buying a house, there are many equally important considerations, such as price, location, number and size of rooms, layout and size of garden. Sometimes the outside appearance of a house is not exactly what you had in mind. Remember, there are many ways of improving the exterior, including colourful paintwork; planting the front garden or tidying up the outside space; replacing broken drainpipes; and changing the front door. If you are selling your house, do remember that first impressions play an important role, and that the front of a house is a reflection of the inside.

Traditional stone-clad cottages, mock-Tudor, semi-detached properties and New England-style, clapboard houses are just a few of the many different types of exteriors. Illustrated opposite are some examples of typical British architectural styles.

BRITISH ARCHITECTURAL STYLES

Victorian terrace

New build with integral garage

Country cottage

Edwardian terrace

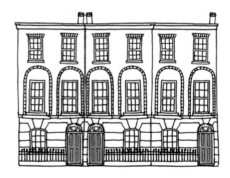

Georgian terrace

1930s suburban semi

CROSS-SECTION OF A HOUSE

Your house is the most expensive thing you own, so it is essential to keep it in a good state of repair. Regular maintenance will help to prevent major problems occurring.

Although this book is principally concerned with interior design, it is worth remembering that you can increase the value of your house by caring for and decorating its exterior. External maintenance of any home is also fundamental in terms of providing you with a warm, comfortable home that works well. If the outside of the house is in a bad state of repair, it's no good spending time and money on the inside, as decorative elements could be impaired – the lovely expensive wallpaper that was fitted in the bedroom might start to fall off if damp penetrates, maybe via cracked render on walls.

Before deciding to buy a house or apartment, it is advisable to have it checked out by a professional surveyor to make sure that it is structurally sound. However, make some spot checks yourself before spending money on a survey. And a list of salient points will also help when it comes to looking after your existing home, as it can be difficult to be objective about possible improvements (see opposite).

USEFUL SPOT CHECKS

- ▶ Cracks or bulges in walls can indicate movement of structure, but small cracks are not serious.
- ▶ Look for poor or crumbly pointing on brickwork. Does it need repointing?
- ▶ Are there any rotten windows or cracked sills, and does the woodwork need to be repainted? Roof lights or dormer windows often get overlooked because they can be hard to reach.
- ▶ Condition of the roof – are there any missing tiles or slates and do all the tiles or slates match?
- ▶ Inspect the chimneys for faults. Heavy television aerials attached to chimneys can weaken them.
- ▶ Downpipes and guttering – are they firmly attached to walls and in good order?
- ▶ Check to see if the house has a damp-proof course.
- ▶ Make sure that any porch or extension is adequately connected to the main structure.

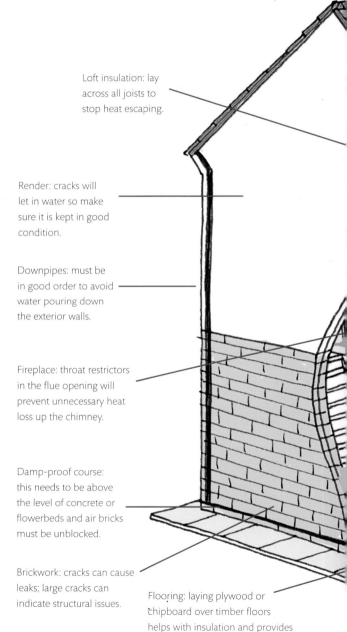

Loft insulation: lay across all joists to stop heat escaping.

Render: cracks will let in water so make sure it is kept in good condition.

Downpipes: must be in good order to avoid water pouring down the exterior walls.

Fireplace: throat restrictors in the flue opening will prevent unnecessary heat loss up the chimney.

Damp-proof course: this needs to be above the level of concrete or flowerbeds and air bricks must be unblocked.

Brickwork: cracks can cause leaks; large cracks can indicate structural issues.

Flooring: laying plywood or chipboard over timber floors helps with insulation and provides a base for tiles and carpet.

Water tank and pipes: if you have them, make sure they are insulated.

Chimney: susceptible to leaks so make sure brickwork and flashing is in good condition.

Roof: loose or poorly fitting tiles can let in water. Check regularly.

Flashing: must be well fitted to make sure water does not penetrate vulnerable parts of the roof.

Guttering: needs to be clear from leaves and other debris to avoid overflows.

Extractor vent: extractor fans in bathrooms help to reduce condensation and the chance of mildew developing.

Windows: double glazing helps insulate against heat loss and noise.

Window sills: fill cracks to avoid draughts and leaks.

Cavity wall insulation: will reduce heat loss considerably.

Flowerbeds: can encourage damp when positioned against walls.

Door: should not be below ground level to prevent rotting.

CARING FOR EXTERIORS

Treat the exterior of your house as you would the interior, making sure
that the various elements complement each other, are in good condition,
and are true to the style of the house.

WALLS

- **Attractive brickwork** should simply be put in good
  order and left at that – don't be tempted to paint it.
  Brickwork should be repointed when necessary; it will
  not only look smarter, but it can also remove the main
  cause of damp penetration. Make sure that the new
  mortar matches the old.

- **Rendered walls** (from roughcast to smooth stucco),
  require more maintenance than brickwork. Today,
  cement-based render is common, but unlike traditional
  lime-based renders, such as stucco, it is non-porous
  and rigid so doesn't allow for any movement or for
  the walls to 'breathe'. Cracks can appear, moisture
  penetrates, causing the wall to deteriorate and plaster
  to fall off. Repair cracks with the same type of render
  as the original.

- **Pebbledash** is a feature of interwar housing – not
  particularly appealing, but very durable and largely
  maintenance-free. If it looks dreary next to dull
  woodwork, brush it down with plenty of water and
  paint the woodwork white. Alternatively, you can
  paint pebbledash.

- **Timber cladding** is found on many types of exteriors,
  old and new. Some timber, cedar, for example, is best
  left to weather to a silvery grey shade, whereas other
  timber-clad walls are painted. The use of weather-
  boarded walls (or clapboarded walls) is essentially an
  effective way of sealing a house against the weather.

- **Painted walls** (rendered or timber-clad) will need to
  be repainted at some point. Whatever the surface,
  always prepare well. Thoroughly clean the surface,
  removing dirt, moss, lichen, flaking and powdering
  paint. You may need to use a stabilising treatment prior
  to painting – check with paint manufacturers. Use paint
  that is appropriate for the surface.

- **Synthetic renders** are also available – they boast low
  maintenance and are available in a range of colours
  and textures. Similarly UPVC, wood-effect cladding

will provide a maintenance-free surface. On existing
properties, always check to see if planning permission
is required before considering any cladding.

ROOFS AND CHIMNEYS

- **Looking after a roof** is key to maintaining a property –
  if the roof leaks it can cause all sorts of damage. Mostly,
  slipped, missing, cracked or broken slate or clay tiles
  are the reason for leaks. When repairing roofs, ensure
  that new work is consistent with the old and check that
  every section of roof drains to a gutter.

- **Chimneys** are usually constructed from brick, and, because of their elevated position, are susceptible to the effects of bad weather. While you can check to see if you have any leaning chimneys, eroded pointing or damaged pots, it is advisable to get a specialist to do the work.

WINDOWS

- **Wooden frames** last indefinitely if they are properly maintained. It is nearly always possible to repair wooden windows. However, neglected paintwork and missing putty can lead to wet rot. Before repairing windows with wet rot, always eradicate the source of the dampness.
- **If you replace windows**, make sure that they fit in with the characteristics of the house. UPVC, wood or metal windows are available in a variety of styles to suit your house. However, a UPVC sash window does not work as well as a wooden one in a Victorian terrace, for example.

FRONT DOORS

- **The front door** is the focus of attention for visitors – it is a place to make a statement. This may take the form of a splash of colour against a plain façade. It may be that the door is embellished with stained glass, or quality fittings.
- **If you have to replace glass** in a front door, ensure that you comply with British Standards. (**Note:** you do not have to replace old glass that is still intact.)
- **A solid front door** is important for reasons of security.

FRONT OF THE HOUSE

- **Plastic downpipes and gutters** are virtually maintenance-free; in addition, they can be painted to fit in with the colour of the walls. From time to time, check that gutters and rainwater heads are not clogged up with leaves. This can cause overflows that can in turn cause damp to penetrate walls.
- **Creeping plants**, such as ivy, should be removed. Roots can penetrate joints and can dislocate bricks and cause render to crack.
- **Dustbins** and recycling bins can be housed in brick-built or wooden sheds and outhouses.
- **If your TV aerial** has to be outside, try to place it in a discreet position. Always make sure that they are well fitted and adequately supported.

STARTING WITH THE INSIDE BASICS

FIND YOUR STYLE

The way you design your home says just as much about you as the clothes you wear. This is your space: as well as being perfectly suited to your lifestyle, it should look beautiful and make you feel good, too.

What is your interior style? Perhaps you can give a snappy, one-word answer straight away. Perhaps you have to think for a while. Or maybe you just don't know. Finding a style is an opportunity to explore the way in which you want to live. It is not about fitting into a set of rules, but about exploring what works best for you, what suits the structure of your home, and what elements will bring you happiness on a daily basis.

The best way to start is by thinking about who lives in the house and how you use it. Which rooms do you spend most time in, and at what times of day? Where do you need spaces that are light and bright, and what areas can be cosy and intimate? Are you formal, or more relaxed? How tidy are you (be honest)? Consider the architecture of your home, and its location, too – an Art Deco seaside home suits a different style to, say, a Georgian townhouse, while a rural cottage lends itself to yet another look.

Architecture aside, however, you should also think about your own taste and personality. When you flick through a book or magazine, watch a television programme or walk round the shops, what styles appeal the most? Do you yearn for a romantic retreat, full of ornaments and pretty colours, or hanker after a tough, industrial look in minimal black and grey? Are you thoroughly modern, retro-obsessed or a lover of antiques and period details? Perhaps you are inspired by foreign travels or a special place that you once visited. Do not worry: this is not a test, and you can't get the answers wrong. Relax and enjoy the process, because once you start to define your style you are on the way to creating a unique vision of how you want to live.

A fabulous original feature. From the mid-1880s, cast-iron fireplaces adorned with elaborate, colourful tiles were becoming highly fashionable.

PERIOD DETAILS

If you are lucky enough to live in an older home with original architectural details, it is worth ensuring that they are restored to their full glory, and complemented by a well-chosen decorative scheme. While an exact replica of a particular period style may be slightly over the top, a few retro or antique pieces could be just the thing to enhance the overall character of your home. On the other hand, you may wish to contrast your period details with ultra-modern furniture. Either way, finding out about the history of your home is always a rewarding endeavour, and will stand you in good stead when you are making design decisions.

PERIOD CHARACTER

Georgian sash windows
Fashionable houses featured double-hung sash windows. After 1709, they were inset to prevent fire spreading.

Regency ironwork
Cast-iron features in classically inspired geometric forms and floral designs were common.

Georgian internal door
A six-panel door such as this, featuring a moulded doorcase, is typical of a late Georgian property.

Georgian cornice
The acanthus leaf pattern was hugely popular in the late Georgian period.

Victorian internal door
A four-panelled, wooden door like this is a type commonly found in modest Victorian houses.

Victorian ceiling rose
Ornate ceiling roses make a wonderful feature in many Victorian homes.

Victorian fireplace
From the late 1850s, cast-iron fireplaces were mass-produced, usually with ornamental tiled panels.

Victorian letterbox
Letterboxes became common after the introduction of the Penny Post in 1840. This one is also a knocker.

Edwardian balusters
New technology made square-cut shapes such as these less expensive to produce.

Edwardian fireplace
Stained pine has replaced Victorian dark oak for this Tudor-style surround. Patterned tiles were also popular.

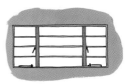

1930s window
Long metal windows with two opening casements and fixed central sections were common in 1930s modern houses.

1930s door
Doors often combined metal and glass, and the sunray motif is typical of the period.

GLOBAL INFLUENCES

When it comes to design inspiration, we literally have a whole world
of styles from which to choose.

For many people, decorating in a global style means finding a way to incorporate a special piece brought back from a trip abroad – an item of furniture, a colourful rug or a length of unusual fabric – into an overall scheme. Or it could simply be the desire to evoke the atmosphere of a region by choosing specific colours, patterns and textures. This is an opportunity to search auctions, antiques and charity shops and jumble sales for interesting pieces, or spend foreign holidays in souks and flea markets, workshops and rug shops, soaking up the atmosphere in order to replicate it back home. Even if you are on a tight budget, just one or two inexpensive pieces can create a eye-catching display.

When decorating with a global perspective, you can mix and match as much as you like. Just as historical styles do not begin and end at exact times, so global styles tend not to stop at man-made political boundaries. By exploring the wealth of beautiful crafts and furnishings from around the world, you can create your own individual and appealing look.

SCANDINAVIAN
- ▶ Light, bright and airy.
- ▶ Pale colours with dashes of heartening red, green, yellow and mid-blue.
- ▶ Sheer and checked fabrics.
- ▶ Painted wooden furniture.
- ▶ Curly metal chandeliers and mirror-backed sconces.

CLASSIC FRENCH
- ▶ Smart and sophisticated.
- ▶ Glass chandeliers, curly metalwork and oversized mirrors.
- ▶ Rich fabrics with arabesque patterns of ribbons, garlands and swags.
- ▶ Neutral colours such as grey, taupe and eau de nil, combined with stronger shades such as burgundy and navy.

INDIAN

- ▶ Relaxed, comfortable and eclectic.
- ▶ Saturated shades, including pink, crimson, orange, saffron, lime and purple.
- ▶ Luscious fabrics, sometimes including metal threads.
- ▶ Dark wood furniture, embellished with brass.
- ▶ Beaten metal, earthenware and wooden lattice-work accessories.
- ▶ Intricate patterns, especially featuring the boteh, the teardrop shape featured in paisley.

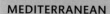

MEDITERRANEAN

- ▶ Simple, vibrant and informal.
- ▶ Vivid colours, including earthy terracottas, sunny yellows and geranium reds.
- ▶ Hand-crafted furnishings.
- ▶ Multicoloured, flat-woven rugs.
- ▶ Striped, checked and floral fabrics.

NORTH AFRICAN

- ▶ Richly decorative and sensual.
- ▶ Geometric and floral patterns.
- ▶ Warm colours such as mustard, ruby, saffron, emerald and orange.
- ▶ Intricate and colourful tilework.
- ▶ Floor cushions and bolsters.

THE MODERN APPROACH

Do you yearn for simplicity or adore a cosy, colourful look?
Now is the time to express your individuality.

If you don't plan to include historical or global references into your decorating scheme, you may wonder just what is your style. Well, the answer is that the modern home can be anything you want it to be – pared-down and minimal, rustic and natural, pretty and nostalgic – but above all, it should be your vision, your look, your very own style.

No matter what your type of property, or where you live, pulling together a modern look that suits you perfectly is not necessarily difficult, time-consuming or expensive – it may simply be a question of re-thinking what goes where, giving a lick of paint to one or two key pieces, and adding some inexpensive accessories. The aim is to create an impression of visual coherence so it all just feels 'right'. Think about colours, patterns, textures, furniture, fabrics and lighting (they all come later in this book). There are plenty of styles to choose from, all of them a pleasure to live with and easy on the eye. Now it's up to you.

INDUSTRIAL
▶ Minimal yet rugged.
▶ Monochrome colours, especially black, white and grey.
▶ Brick, concrete, metal and glass.
▶ Sleek furniture with simple outlines.
▶ Salvaged lighting.

SIMPLE
▶ Fuss-free and functional.
▶ Off-whites combined with stronger colours.
▶ Natural materials – wood, slate, wicker, wool and cotton.
▶ Simple, timeless furniture.
▶ Plain and striped fabrics; plain white tiles.
▶ Tongue-and-groove panelling on walls.

COUNTRY

- ▶ Comfortable, charming and timeless.
- ▶ Floral fabrics for soft furnishings.
- ▶ The colours of a country garden.
- ▶ A farmhouse kitchen (or at least a wooden dresser to give a country flavour).
- ▶ Traditional crockery such as blue-and-white striped or spongeware.
- ▶ Block-printed wallpapers.
- ▶ Baskets, Lloyd Loom furniture and cosy throws on beds, chairs and sofas.

ROMANTIC

- ▶ Floaty and feminine.
- ▶ Droplet chandeliers and etched glass.
- ▶ Lace and sheer fabrics.
- ▶ Pale colours and faded patterns.
- ▶ Delicate metal furniture.
- ▶ Vintage teacups, glass and picture frames.

RETRO

- ▶ Individual and eye-catching.
- ▶ Statement pieces from past eras.
- ▶ Plastic kitsch or mid-century modern cool.
- ▶ Lava lamps, geometric fabric and coloured glass.
- ▶ Iconic furniture and/or inexpensive and interesting finds.

YOUR STYLE – MAKING IT WORK

You don't need deep pockets to create a great interior, just some time,
effort and a little thoughtful ingenuity.

In real life, very few of us live in
the sort of homes one sees in
magazines or on the TV. Unless you
have spent a fortune and acquired
all of your furniture in one go,
you're likely to have an assortment
of things that don't quite match
– a dining table inherited from
grandparents, an antique bookshelf
bought at auction, a nice bed from
a high-street store, a retro chair
you found in a charity shop. It can
be hard to see how such diverse
items can be put together to create
a coherent decorative scheme.
But with some basic principles, a
dash of design inspiration and a
burst of enthusiasm, you will soon
be able to combine old and new,
antique and modern, vintage and
contemporary with aplomb – and in
a way that suits both your style and
your budget.

A TEN-POINT PLAN FOR MIX-AND-MATCH INTERIORS

1 Assess your furniture and how it works in each room. What goes well together and what sticks out like a sore thumb?

2 Move furniture around, sell or give it away as appropriate. Start looking everywhere for items you are short of – from the high street to auction houses, antiques shops to car boot sales.

3 Try to limit the variation in heights of furnishings – tops of bookcases, sofas, tables and so on. The room will appear more unified.

4 Scale is important. A pair of sofas, for example, work best if they are in proportion rather than one being tall and overstuffed and the other low and lean.

5 Choose timeless, well-made designs. It doesn't matter what period they come from (within reason): they will work well with other pieces.

6 Transform pieces that don't suit your scheme. A lick of paint or a new loose cover can work wonders.

7 Co-ordinate colours and patterns and create a pleasing variety of textures.

8 Keep flooring simple: this provides a calm backdrop for everything else.

9 Avoid too many 'star' pieces that distract the eye. One or two wow-factor items are enough.

10 Keep experimenting – you may not get it right first time, but it's worth trying again. 'If in doubt, take it out' is a good rule of thumb.

Where to find style inspiration

Inspiration is all around us, but everyone needs a little nudge in the right direction from time to time. Here are just a few ideas.

- Decorating and furniture showrooms.
- Markets.
- Books, magazines and catalogues.
- The architecture and history of your home.
- Other people's houses.
- Films and TV programmes.
- Shops, restaurants and hotels.
- Art galleries and museums.
- The world around you – rural or urban.
- Your own wardrobe.
- Blogs and digital magazines.
- A favourite piece of furniture that you already own.

INTERNAL LAYOUT

No matter how big or small your home, it's time to maximise
every square inch, creating a comfortable sense of space
and using every room to its full potential.

In any home, large or tiny, the best spaces are those which are harmoniously clutter-free – practical rooms, easy and enjoyable to use every day, and good-looking to boot. Even large rooms suffer if you haven't sorted out adequate storage, the furniture is badly arranged, or if the lighting is inadequate. The smaller the room, the more noticeable these problems become, and there is no doubt that tiny spaces require even more careful planning than usual.

That said, just because a room is small or awkwardly shaped, it doesn't mean that it can't be great. With pleasant proportions, the right colours and a shrewd choice of furnishings, you can turn a tiny or a tricky room into a wonderful gem.

There are two ways of dealing with problematic rooms: by altering them physically, or by using visual tricks to make them appear bigger, smaller, higher, lower, longer or wider.

Vertical stripes can emphasise ceiling height in a tall room or give the illusion of space in a room with a lower ceiling.

PHYSICAL SOLUTIONS

▶ Consider the big options – knocking through, raising the ceiling, adding a mezzanine, for example.

▶ Conventional hinged doors take up a lot of space in a small room. Can you swap them for sliding or bi-fold doors? Or you could remove the door entirely.

▶ Clear every bit of clutter you possibly can. Then sort out your storage. High-level storage can be the answer when space is tight.

▶ Folding, stacking, hideaway, compact and dual-purpose furniture are all good space-saving options.

▶ If possible, fit underfloor heating and get rid of space-guzzling radiators.

▶ In rooms with low ceilings, replace dangling pendant lights with inset spots or table lamps.

VISUAL TRICKS

▶ In narrow rooms, fake a feeling of width by using horizontal patterns on walls or floors. Similarly, vertical stripes can make low-ceilinged rooms appear taller. A dark ceiling makes an overly high ceiling seem lower.

▶ In a small room, use the same colour on the walls, floors and ceiling. Blurring those boundaries increases the feeling of space.

▶ Light-reflecting paints are an inexpensive way to boost a sense of space.

▶ Being able to see more of the floor makes a room seem less crowded, so use wall-hung furniture in appropriate places.

▶ Furniture on slender legs also shows more floor space – giving the illusion of a larger area. The same goes for anything made from glass or acrylic.

▶ Use mirrors and other reflective surfaces as much as possible in a small or dark room.

Fitting in a home office

We all need a workspace somewhere at home, whether you work from home full time or are simply answering the odd email. As long as you can find room for a small desk (or even a shelf in an alcove, set at the right height) with some storage and a plug socket or two nearby, you are well on your way. Here are some ideas:

▶ Under the stairs.
▶ In the loft.
▶ In a large cupboard.
▶ On the landing.
▶ In a spare bedroom.
▶ A corner of the bedroom, living room or kitchen.
▶ The garage or garden shed.
▶ A dedicated building in the garden.

Create a workspace in an area that might otherwise be wasted. Folding chairs can be put away when not in use, saving masses of space.

ZONING AND FLOW

Don't take your home for granted. With some clever thinking you can configure your space so that it suits you and your family perfectly.

When it comes to thinking about how we use our homes, designers might talk about zoning and flow, but what's important is this: how does your house suit you and your family? Is it easy or awkward to live in?

Start by considering the house as a whole, trying to see each room as a blank canvas. Are you really making the best use of the layout? Sometimes we follow preconceived ideas, or those imposed on the house by previous owners, when really we need to change things around – turn a spare bedroom into a home office, or make a seldom-used dining room a teenagers' hangout. It could make sense to put a laundry room near the bedrooms rather than in its traditional place by the kitchen, or turn a first-floor bedroom into a sitting room to make the most of lovely views.

Old houses can be more spacious than new-builds, but do offer particular challenges as they can often be a warren of small rooms, rarely have enough bathrooms and never have enough plug sockets. Can you convert a box room into an ensuite? If you extended across a side return, could you create a family-friendly open-plan living space? And what will happen if you have a baby, your children leave home, an elderly relative comes to stay, or you change career and need a fully functioning home office?

Open-plan kitchen/dining spaces are perfect for families and entertaining.

If possible, future-proof your home so that it's flexible enough to deal with whatever life throws at it.

If the big projects (extensions, loft conversions, going open-plan) are not possible or necessary, there are plenty of smaller changes that can help streamline your home. Such relatively simple alterations as re-hanging a door, moving a radiator, enlarging a window or adding wall lights and extra plug sockets can turn an awkward home into one that's tailor-made for you. Make the effort now – you definitely won't regret it.

In the work area of this open-plan living space, the shelving has been cleverly angled to make the most of the shape of the walls.

Designing a room layout

▶ Measure the room as carefully as possible, and draw a scaled-down plan of it (as if you were looking from above) on graph paper. Draw in the current positions of windows, doors, built-in cupboards, radiators, plug sockets and light fittings.
▶ Think about whether all the architectural elements are in the right place. Perhaps it would help if you took down a wall, moved a radiator, re-hung the door so it opens the other way, or added some extra plug sockets?
▶ If you are working on a bathroom or kitchen, work out where the pipes run. Will you need to alter them?
▶ On a separate sheet of paper, but using the same scale as the room plan, sketch the approximate shape of your furniture (again, as if you were looking at them from above). Cut them out and place them on the plan. Do they fit well into the space? Is there enough 'activity room' around them (space to swing your legs out of bed; elbow room around a basin)?
▶ Move the furniture around or re-assess its shape and size as necessary. Once everything is in the right place, you should have the basics of a functional and comfortable room.

Grouping the furniture at one end of this long room creates a cosy space for relaxing.

ACCESS ALL AREAS

There's no doubt that huge, airy and bright open-plan spaces are wonderfully appealing. But just how do you create the perfect open-plan, multi-use, family-friendly space?

1 If you work from home or really value your privacy, then keep at least one living space where you can shut yourself away. Alternatively, folding doors, or a simple screen, could do the trick.

2 When creating an open-plan kitchen, dining and living area, you will either need a separate utility room or a super-quiet dishwasher and washing machine. A low-decibel extractor over the cooker is vital, too.

3 In any room that has more than one function, the furniture needs to blend from one area to another. Create an overall style that works as well for comfy seating as it does for kitchen units.

4 Delineate areas within the open-plan space by varying paint colours and using clever lighting – different circuits are best, controlled by switches or dimmers.

5 Either 'zone' different areas by varying the flooring, or go for an all-purpose hard or vinyl floor that can be softened with rugs where necessary.

6 Open-plan rooms have less wall space for storage, so you have to be clever with your clobber. Consider open shelves that double as a room divider, seating that doubles as storage and fitted furniture that uses every inch of height or quirky corner that you have.

7 Open-plan, multi-purpose rooms can lack focus. A feature wall or large work of art may be the answer.

8 Conventional furniture can look out of place in a large, open space – you may need to buy larger-than-average pieces.

The carpet and paint colours make the two areas of this long, thin room co-ordinate seamlessly.

This large living space is divided into living, dining, play and work areas.

Knocking down walls

Before you get out the sledgehammer, make sure that the wall you are knocking down isn't loadbearing. If it is, you will have to insert a beam over the new opening (employ a structural engineer to do the calculations). Either way, you must also check with your local planning authority whether the work is subject to building regulations.

CONNECTING SPACES

Halls and landings often get overlooked, yet your hall is like a handshake: the introduction to your house, while the landing is a vital linking area. Think of both as if they were rooms in their own right, and give them the attention they deserve.

Increase the feeling of space in a narrow hallway by using pale colours and large mirrors. Keep the space as clear as possible by adding slim storage furniture, hung on walls where possible. Welcoming lighting that leads the eye into your home is important. Avoid wall lights as they can be obstacles, but think pretty chandeliers or perhaps a series of contemporary recessed ceiling lights.

Even on the smallest landing you can use walls to display art or photographs, or maybe hang a set of slender bookshelves. In a slightly larger area you could have a small ottoman, a trunk or even a handy desk, tallboy or chest of drawers. Bright lights are important so that you don't trip on the stairs. Lastly, make sure your landing's decorative scheme works well when doorways to other rooms are open.

FLOOR PLANS

Planning makes perfect. Before you decide on flooring, wall coverings,
colours and furnishings and, most importantly, before you go to any expense,
it is a good idea to design your room layout.

Good design is predominantly common sense. The first thing you need to do is to think about how you want the room to be used, not only for your family, but also for your friends.

It is wise not to rush into things. Having a small-scale plan of your room drawn out on graph paper is a great help when organising the room (see below). You can even measure your existing furniture and cut out shapes to scale, also using graph paper. This will allow you to play around with various solutions before making any final decisions.

When you have taken all things into consideration and the layout is almost settled, make a final check to test the viability of the plan. Ask yourself whether you are making the best use of the space, and always think about what suits your way of life.

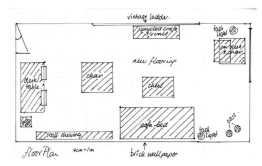

*Using graph paper to map the
features of your room will help
you get an accurate idea of
how the layout will work.*

DRAWING TO SCALE

Getting your plan down on paper will give you a clearer idea of the space in and proportions of your room. There's no arguing with accurate measurements, and that's what drawing to scale is all about.

Begin by making a rough diagram of the room, showing the approximate shape and size, together with the position of doors, windows, chimney breasts, alcoves, fireplaces, radiators and built-in cupboards or storage. Using a tape measure or extendable wooden rule, measure the length and width of the room, including the dimensions of its features. Put these figures onto your rough drawing. To convert the rough sketch into a scale drawing, use a fixed ratio that translates your actual dimensions into ones of manageable proportions. Decide on a scale of conversion, for example, 2.5cm to 1m (1in to 3¼ft), which means that every 1m (3¼ft) of your room will convert to 2.5cm (1in) on your scaled drawing. Working to a metric scale on centimetre-square graph paper, and to an imperial scale on ¼in-square graph paper, draw your plan, adding all of the features in their correct position. Take a number of copies of your plan so that you can begin to try out your ideas, maybe by drawing in a furniture layout – but make sure you work to the same scale and measure accurately.

USING COMPUTERS

Professional architectural drawings and design plans are constructed with the help of computer-aided (CAD) systems. Why not use a computer to help you design your room layout? All you need is a simple programme that, with a little practise, will enable you to construct a room layout. Look up CAD for interior design on the Internet and find a programme suitable for home use. In most cases the software incorporates examples of rooms, furniture and fittings that can be selected and moved around to fit your dimensions and specifications.

FLOOR PLANS

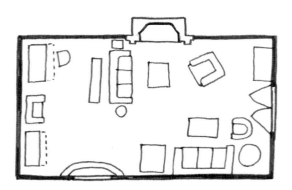

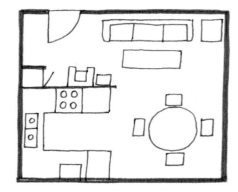

Living room
Group chairs and sofas in distinct areas or around focal points. Make sure there are tables within easy reach. Place desks near windows for natural light.

Open-plan area
Create separate living and eating areas so that the functions of the room are clear. You also need to be able to move easily between each area.

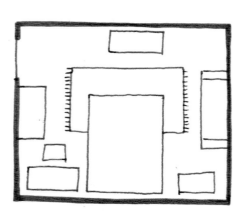

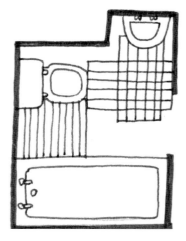

Bedroom
The bed is the focal point, so place it where it is most accessible and can be viewed to its best advantage. Make sure your view from the bed is the best available, too.

Bathroom
Even in a small bathroom there has to be sufficient room between the different elements; ideally you need over 1m (3ft) between the WC and the facing wall and between the basin and the open door.

FLOORS

From soft wool to warm wood, classic carpet to fashionable rubber,
flooring is fundamental to the look and feel of a room.

These days, almost anything goes for flooring: gone are the days of tiles in the kitchen, carpet in the bedroom and floorboards in the living room – you can have mosaic in your living room, rubber in your kitchen and marble in your home office, if you so wish. Before aesthetics though, it comes down to practicalities – the amount of wear and tear the floor will take. So put your toughest, most durable flooring in the hall and living room, and a more delicate type in a spare bedroom, for example. For kitchens, bathrooms, utility rooms and conservatories, there is another consideration: how well it will withstand spills, splashes and general humidity. Choose the right flooring for your space and it will not only look good but also last and last.

WHAT LIES BENEATH

The success of any flooring depends on the sub-floor underneath. For example, if you lay carpets and sheet flooring, such as vinyl or lino, straight onto floorboards, after a while you will begin to see the parallel lines showing through. You need to cover the boards first with a thin sheet of hardboard or plywood. (What's more, a good-quality underlay makes a huge difference as to how long carpet will last.) If you plan to lay heavy stone tiles, the sub-floor may need reinforcing – if in doubt, check with your builder or a structural engineer. Tiles of any type are best laid onto a dry, smooth, level, concrete sub-floor – you can apply a self-levelling compound, if necessary.

TYPES OF FLOORING

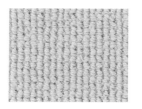

Carpet
Warm, soft and quiet underfoot, carpet is a classic choice. The downside is that stains can be hard to remove.

Natural fibres
Sisal, coir, jute, seagrass and rush all come under this heading. They are available in a range of colours, weaves and textures.

Vinyl
Available in both sheet and tile form, vinyl is relatively easy to lay. Warm and soft underfoot; it is also water-resistant.

Linoleum
Modern lino is durable, stain-resistant and easy to clean, as well as being environmentally friendly.

Solid wood
Timeless and durable, solid wood flooring (boards or parquet) is extremely practical, although it is not a cheap option.

Laminate floors
Varies from inexpensive – a photo of wood bonded to a chipboard base – to quality 'engineered' versions.

Ceramic and porcelain
Heat- and water-resistant, durable and easy to clean, but this flooring is cold underfoot.

Stone and slate
Sandstone, limestone, slate and granite are all luxurious choices. They can be porous, so check whether they require sealing.

Bamboo
Fast-growing and self-regenerating, bamboo is environmentally friendly and easy to clean. It is good for humid areas, too.

Marble
The epitome of luxury, with a beautiful grain and attractive colouring. But it is cold and hard underfoot.

Rubber
In the form of tiles or sheets, rubber is warm and soft, yet durable and water-resistant. A textured design gives better grip.

Leather
Expensive and unusual, leather floors require regular buffing or waxing and develop a patina over the years.

WOOD

Wooden floors are beautiful, hardwearing and just get
better and better as they age.

SOLID WOOD

Wooden flooring is available as boards in a variety
of widths, strips (less than 10cm/4in wide), blocks
(extremely strong, laid in patterns such as herringbone
and basketweave) and parquet (like blocks, but thinner,
see below). Oak and pine are classic, while beech, ash and
maple are practical and attractive, too. Exotic hardwoods
such as wenge, teak, merbau and iroko make a dramatic
impression, while bamboo (technically a grass, but a
sustainable alternative nevertheless) has an individual
look. Solid wooden floors can be sanded, painted, limed,
stained, waxed or varnished.

ENGINEERED WOOD

This is sometimes called multi-layer or, confusingly,
laminated wood, and is made either from several layers of
solid timber or else a thin layer of solid timber attached
to a cheaper base made from MDF, plywood, chipboard
or softwood. Solid-wood engineered boards are cross-
bonded for stability (meaning they won't warp or move,
which solid timber is prone to), making them a good
choice with underfloor heating.

LAMINATE

Made from a resin-impregnated decorative paper surface
layer printed with photographs of real wood, bonded to
a thin MDF or chipboard core. With cheaper versions it is
easy to spot the pattern repeat, plus they're less durable.
More expensive laminate flooring can be incredibly tough
– look for a long guarantee.

PARQUET

Originally a French 17th-century flooring technique,
parquet became affordable (thanks to mechanisation) in
the early 20th century and remained fashionable until the
1930s, when carpet and lino began to take precedence.
Made up of hardwood blocks laid in a geometric pattern
– such as herringbone, basketweave and chevron –
parquet has a distinctive and timeless look.

HOW TO SAND FLOORBOARDS

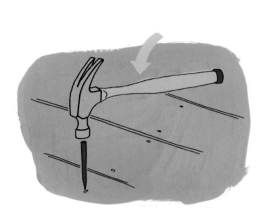

Mend or replace any damaged boards. Fill any large gaps with thin slivers of matching timber. Hammer any protruding nail heads below the surface of the board. Remove furniture and soft furnishings, seal the door and open the windows – there will be a lot of dust.

Use a drum sander fitted with coarse paper for the main floor area, sanding diagonally from corner to corner. Start with the drum tilted back off the floor, switch it on and then gently lower it down. Guide it in a slow, steady line. Don't allow it to stop, or it will gouge a hollow in your boards. At the end of the run, tilt it back, switch it off and let the drum stop before you lower it.

Work in parallel, slightly overlapping runs, and when you have finished the first diagonal, sweep up and then do the opposite diagonal. Sweep again, then change to medium sandpaper and work parallel to the boards. Use a fine-grade sandpaper for a final, parallel sand.

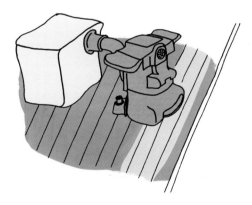

Use a disc sander for the edges and corners, working from coarse to fine paper as before. A scraper or power drill sanding attachment will get into any areas the edging sander can't reach. Vacuum, then finish by wiping the floor with a cloth dampened with white spirit.

FINISHING WOOD FLOORS

Your choice of finish will depend on both practicality and style. Halls and kitchens need hardwearing finishes but bedrooms less so. You will also want your floor to look good and contribute to the atmosphere of the room.

SEALED WOOD FLOORS

A sealed floor is one that has been treated with a clear coating that allows the grain of the wood to be seen, and which dries to form a protective finish. This 'clear coating' can sit on the surface or penetrate into the wood. Coatings can be in the form of a clear varnish (solvent or water based – matt, satin or gloss) or a specialist oil or wax. For new wooden floors or freshly sanded floorboards, it is preferable to seal rather than stain them, so that the natural beauty of the wood can be seen.

STAINED WOOD FLOORS

Wood stains in various forms (see right) are durable. Finishes come in a wide range of colours – translucent and opaque. Generally, they are used to add colour as well as protection. Use a stain if you want to change the look of the wood. For instance, a dark oak stain could be applied over a light-coloured pine floor to give a different effect. Wood stains are also ideal for covering blemishes in poor-quality timber.

PAINTED WOOD FLOORS

Paint is one of the quickest ways to transform a room. If you paint a wooden floor in a colour that complements the rest of your furnishings, you will not only have a completely new floor, but also a hardwearing and practical one. It is a relatively inexpensive way of grounding a room and unifying patchy floorboards.

Types of finish

There are a multitude of products for floor finishes, but generally they belong to one of two categories: those that penetrate the wood and those that sit on the surface to form a protective film.

- **Oil:** Traditional oil, such as Danish or teak oil, protects and seals the wood by penetrating the surface. Oil gives a natural-looking and mellow quality.
- **Wood stain:** This is used to change the colour of wood and is available in two forms: a stain that seeps into the wood (which can then be sealed with either clear varnish or wax); and a coloured varnish that will stain the wood in one operation.
- **Wax:** This can be used on bare wood or as a finish for stained or sealed floors. Available as a paste or liquid, it protects and enhances the qualities of wood.
- **Varnish:** Solvent or water based, these are available in a range of sheen levels, from matt to high gloss. Most clear varnishes darken the wood to some degree.
- **Paint:** Floor paint is available in a wide range of colours. On bare wood, apply a primer followed by an undercoat (see opposite). Floor paint dries to a hard finish and is hardwearing.

HOW TO PAINT A WOODEN FLOOR

Preparation

For a good finish it's all about the preparation. The amount of preparation will depend on the condition of your floor. Before painting a wooden floor, make sure that the boards are in good condition, clean, dry and free from dirt and grease. Generally, bare floorboards will only require a light sand. Previously varnished or painted floors will require more work. Remove varnish and as much of the paint as possible. It is essential to remove peeling or blistered paint.

Tip *When sanding, collect the dust; you can mix this with PVA to fill in any gaps, as an alternative to using wood filler.*

Firstly fill in any gaps or cracks with an appropriate wood filler. Sand the floor to remove old finishes. You can use a hand-held electric sander or do it by hand. Once the surface is smooth, use a vacuum cleaner to clear up any dust.

Wash the floor with detergent to remove all traces of dust and leave it to dry. Then, if necessary, apply knotting solution to any knots so that the resin doesn't seep through your paint.

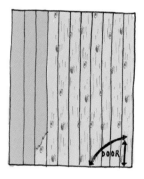

Using a large paintbrush or roller, and painting in the direction of the grain, apply one coat of primer and/or undercoat (suitable for the type of paint you are using). Start from the furthest corner of the room and work on two or three floorboards at a time, moving backwards towards the door. Leave to dry, according to the manufacturer's instructions.

Stir the paint thoroughly. Following the instructions in the previous step (left), apply a first coat of paint. Allow to dry (follow the instructions on the tin). Then apply a second coat of paint and leave to dry. A third coat may be necessary depending on the original surface colour.

SHEET, STONE AND TILES

There is a wide range of alternatives to carpet and timber flooring,
each with its own, unique qualities.

SHEET FLOORING

Softer and warmer than stone or
timber, sheet floorcoverings come
in a surprising variety of colours,
patterns and textures. They are
often available in tile form, too,
and can sometimes be cut into
graphic patterns.

- **Vinyl:** A PVC-based man-made
  material that is hard-wearing,
  slip-resistant, quiet and easy to
  maintain. It tends to be reserved
  for kitchens and bathrooms, but
  can be used anywhere you like,
  and comes in a huge range of
  textures and patterns, many of
  them good imitations of stone,
  wood or ceramic tiles. For a
  contemporary look, designs
  include molten metal, sparkling
  surfaces, abstract prints or
  photographic images.

- **Linoleum:** A traditional material
  made from renewable sources
  – linseed oil, tree resin, wood
  flour, cork powder and pigments
  from natural ingredients. It
  offers a wide range of colours
  and textures, is very durable
  and naturally anti-bacterial and
  biodegradable.

- **Cork:** Often under-rated, cork is
  hardwearing, resilient to water
  and durable. Gone are the orange
  tones familiar from the 1960s –
  cork is now available in a range
  of fashionable shades.

- **Rubber:** Both good-looking and
  practical, rubber is robust, easy

It is always worth trying to restore original flooring like these black and white tiles.

to keep clean and tactile; it is available in smooth or textured designs. The latter are ideal for bathrooms. Rubber floors should be laid professionally.

NATURAL STONE

Sandstone, limestone, granite, marble and terrazzo are expensive floorings that have a beautiful, individual grain and patina, and should last a lifetime – but they are also hard, noisy and cold underfoot.

Stone tiles are available in a range of sizes, from mosaics through to large slabs, and a variety of finishes. In areas that might get wet, such as kitchens or bathrooms, choose a version that is matt or slightly textured – sanded for a rough finish, or riven for an attractive, hand-split effect. Avoid marble in the kitchen, though, as it can stain and corrode, and remember that all stone floorings need to be sealed.

CERAMIC, PORCELAIN AND OTHER TILES

Just like wall tiles, ceramic and porcelain floor tiles are heat- and water-resistant, hardwearing and low maintenance. Thicker than wall tiles, they come in a vast array of shapes, sizes and designs. Unglazed terracotta and quarry tiles are rugged and non-slip but, like any other hard surface; they won't be kind to dropped crockery. Encaustic tiles are a type of patterned ceramic tile very popular in Victorian and Edwardian homes (especially hallways). Distinctive and handsome, they can be restored if they have suffered over the years.

Stone flooring with a riven finish is non-slip but can be rough underfoot.

Period fireplaces often feature original floor tiles, but you can create the same effect using tiles of your choice.

CHOOSING THE RIGHT FLOORING

The floor is the base that supports the other elements in a room. Before making your decision about what flooring to choose, consider price, wear and tear, maintenance, comfort and the atmosphere you want to achieve.

Whatever type of flooring you choose, it will be with you for some time, so bear in mind the financial outlay, which can be considerable. Think about the functions it needs to fulfil. As seen on the previous pages, flooring has properties that suit certain functions. In terms of colour and texture, different materials offer different results. Neutral shades will keep decorative options open and allow for future changes in style. Dark colours and large patterns can make a room seem small, whereas light colours, plain surfaces and small patterns tend to increase the sense of space.

Another consideration is the junction between different types of flooring. In an open-plan living room you can mix different types of flooring to define different areas: for instance, ceramic tiles in the kitchen and wooden flooring in the dining area, but make sure that colours or textures are harmonious. Similarly, when doors are left often open and a vista of rooms opens up off the hall or landing, you will want to make sure there are no jarring transitions between rooms. Try to create flow between rooms and a unity of design.

In some circumstances, you can also connect a ground floor room to a garden or outdoor space. Brick, slate or stone are obvious choices as they can be used inside and out. Brick floors are suitable for ground level only, but depending on the colour, they can be cosy and rustic or cool and chic. Choose bricks that are designed for paving, otherwise the surface will deteriorate quickly.

You might also consider using top quality vinyl flooring, when it is not feasible to use slate or stone. Vinyl sheeting or tiles are available in a huge range of patterns and textures – many of which simulate natural materials.

Tips on laying vinyl sheeting

▶ **Preparation:** Always lay on a firm, flat foundation (see page 38). It is best to leave the vinyl (ideally unrolled) in the room where it is to be laid for 24 hours before laying to make it supple and easier to work with. When measuring, add 5cm (2in) to each edge to allow for final trimming, and measure right up to the centre of any door.

▶ **Making a join:** To join widths of vinyl, lay one sheet over the other (matching any pattern). Using a straightedge and sharp knife, cut through both pieces and remove the waste. Without moving the sheets, fold back the cut edges, apply adhesive or tape and press the join together.

▶ **Cutting around a pedestal:** Lay the sheet up to the pedestal and then fold it back on itself. Using scissors cut a straight line from the edge to the centre of the pedestal. Make triangular cuts around the base of the pedestal working around the curve until the sheet can lie flat on the floor. Make a crease and carefully trim off the excess.

▶ **Doorways:** Working around the door frame, make a series of vertical cuts to the point where the vinyl meets the floor. Cut off the excess, leaving about 5cm (2in) turned up. Press the vinyl into the angle between the floor and door frame, make a crease and trim off the excess. Lastly, make a straight cut across the door opening so that a metal edging strip can be fitted.

▶ **Bonding:** Follow the manufacturer's instructions, as some modern sheet vinyl can be loose-laid. To glue at the perimeter, peel back the edge and spray (or spread) a band of flooring adhesive, or use double-sided floor tape, around the room. In bathrooms it is a good idea to seal the edges.

HOW TO LAY SHEET VINYL

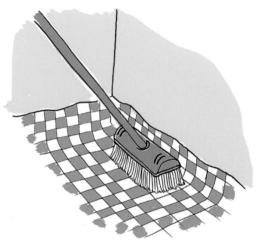

Unroll and lay the vinyl in position. Adjust so that it fits as closely as possible, with the excess running up the skirting board. Use a soft brush or broom to make sure that the vinyl is in close contact with the floor.

Using scissors cut out a triangular notch at each corner, leaving 1.5cm (1in) of the surplus running up the skirting. This will help get the sheet to lie flat. (For external corners, make a straight cut down to the floor, leaving about 5cm/2in turned up. Remove as much waste as possible.)

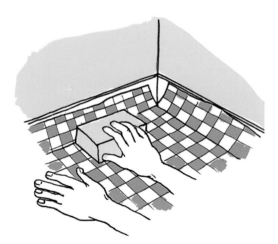

Starting with the longest wall, and using a block of wood (or bolster chisel), press the vinyl into the angle between the floor and skirting board, making a crease. Work around the rest of the walls in the same way.

Align a metal straight edge against the crease running along the longest wall and, using a knife held at a slight angle to the skirting, carefully trim off the excess. Repeat this process around the room.

CARPETS AND RUGS

Soft and comfortable underfoot, carpets and rugs are both practical and beautiful, offering an almost unlimited choice of colour and pattern, and an enormous variety of textures.

WHAT ARE CARPETS AND RUGS MADE OF?

▸ **Wool:** Wool is warm and sumptuous, soft and durable, and does not soil easily.

▸ **Wool blends:** The most common blends are 80% wool with 20% nylon (often recommended as the ideal combination of softness and strength); 80% wool with 10% nylon and 10% polyester; and 50% wool with 50% polypropylene.

▸ **Nylon:** Extremely hardwearing, nylon also takes stain-resistant treatments well.

▸ **Polypropylene:** Resistant to stains and abrasions, polypropylene wears well and is good value for money.

▸ **Polyester:** Stain-resistant, light and bulky, polyester has a lustrous appearance.

TYPES OF CARPET PILE

▸ **Loop:** The pile tufts are left uncut. Avoid if you have pets.

▸ **Cord:** The loops are pulled tight against the backing, giving a very low pile.

▸ **Saxony:** A deeper pile with a soft, sensuous feel and appearance.

▸ **Shag:** Extra-long pile – can catch high heels.

▸ **Twist:** A loop pile that uses yarn with a higher twist than usual to give a coarse, rugged surface. The best types twist two yarn ends tightly together for a very hardwearing carpet.

▸ **Velvet:** A sheared, short pile with a smooth, luxurious finish.

In a room with wooden floors, luxurious, deep-pile rugs will make the living area feel cosy and warm.

WHAT CARPET WHERE?

Carpets are classified for light, moderate, general, heavy and extra heavy domestic use. Select a tough carpet for a hallway: perhaps an 80/20 (wool/nylon) twist classified for heavy domestic; while for a living room a combination of a luxury look with a robust performance, such as a loop or velvet pile, would be best. A spare bedroom carpet could be more delicate – a velvet or Saxony classified for light domestic use, for example. For a seamless look, lay carpet suitable for general use throughout. Carpets are inadvisable in kitchens, and best avoided in bathrooms.

ADD COLOUR AND INTEREST WITH A RUG

A great starting point for a decorative scheme, rugs come in an infinite variety of shapes and sizes, textures and colours, patterns and prices. There is a wonderful range of handmade rugs from around the world, including Indian dhurries, Greek flokatis, Middle Eastern kelims and French aubussons. Modern machine-made rugs can be very attractive, and you can even have a rug woven to your own design.

WALLS

From the simplest of painted walls to vibrant wallpaper or complex tiling, the right wall finish adds atmosphere and creates character in a room.

A plain white wall is not the most exciting decorative idea. However, it could actually be just the thing to show off a colourful collection, or provide a counterpoint to brightly patterned upholstery. Choosing the best wall finish for your space is all about context – and is just as important in terms of decorative effect as selecting colours, fabrics and furnishings. A change of wallcovering can transform cold into cosy, boring into beautiful and out-of-date into ultra cool.

As well as personal choice, there is a practical element, too. While some finishes are delicate, others can protect your walls from bumps, knocks, scrapes, sticky fingers and muddy paws. Some finishes look their best on perfectly straight, smooth walls; others are great at hiding blemishes. Prepare your walls properly and then find your perfect finish. You'll be spoilt for choice.

PREPARING YOUR WALLS

Before you decorate, make sure the surface of your wall is as smooth as possible. The better your preparation, the better the final results. If there is old wallpaper on the walls, it should be stripped off prior to preparing the plaster. Only keep it if it is okay to paint over it. Once stripped, cut out and replace any bulging, loose or crumbling plaster. If you have new plaster it must be properly dried out and, before painting, primed with watered-down emulsion. If you plan to wallpaper over new plaster, you will also need to paint it with sizing solution or watered-down wallpaper paste. If you hang lining paper (go horizontally; it's called cross-lining) it will help to disguise lumpy, bumpy walls before painting or wallpapering.

A large stick-on mural adds to the period feel in this Regency living room.

IDEAS FOR FEATURE WALLS

Roller patterns
With some patience and a steady hand you can create your own wallpaper using patterned paint rollers for a truly individual look.

Bold and beautiful
Wallpaper with an oversized pattern and vivid colours may well be too much for a whole room, but makes a great focal point on just one wall.

All stuck up
Transform your wall with peel-off stickers. They come in all sorts of divine designs from simple shapes to complex illustrations.

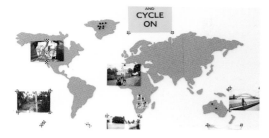

Map of the world
Large maps (old or new) are attractive and educational. Simply paste straight on to the wall. Try sheet music and wrapping paper, too.

Frame wall
Group vintage frames, mirrors and even graphic letters, in all shapes and sizes, to create an intriguing and eye-catching focal point.

Pick up a paintbrush
Try modern, graphic ideas such as bold stripes running horizontally or vertically around the room.

WALLPAPER

Fashionable and fun, wallpaper can be subtle and chic or full of impact.
There is a world of wallpaper choice out there that can introduce pattern,
colour and texture to your room in a variety of textures.

HANGING WALLPAPER: WHERE TO START

Deciding where to start is important. If you begin at the short section of wall above the door frame, you can disguise any pattern mismatch at the point where your last drop meets your first drop without it being noticeable. Or you can start in a corner, and work away from it in both directions. Centre large motifs over the most obvious focal point – a fireplace, above the bed or between two windows.

TYPES OF WALLPAPER

- **Standard decorative wallpapers** are ideal for areas that don't suffer from moisture or severe wear and tear.
- **Washable wallpapers** have a transparent coating, which means they can be wiped down.
- **Vinyls** are durable and easy to apply (they often come pre-pasted). They are all-purpose, but especially suitable for kitchens and bathrooms. Some are textured.
- **Flock wallpapers** feature stencil-like designs with a velvety texture.
- **Embossed wallpapers** feature a raised, textured pattern and are meant to be painted. Blown vinyls are similar.
- **Woodchip wallpaper** contains tiny chips of wood and is usually painted.
- **Foils** are metallic wallcoverings that can vary from a gentle sheen to almost mirror-like.
- **Natural wallcoverings** include materials such as woven grass, silk, wood veneer, hessian and cork, backed with paper. They are often delicate and hard to clean.

How much wallpaper do I need?

To work out how much wallpaper you need to buy you must calculate the area you plan to paper and divide that number by the usable yield per roll of paper (the amount of paper that will actually go on the wall). The usable yield is determined by the type of pattern that appears on the paper.

1 Calculate the **wall area** by multiplying the length and height of each wall and adding these figures together.

2 Calculate the **window area** by multiplying the height and width of each window and adding these figures together.

3 Calculate the **door area** by multiplying the height and width of each door and adding these figures together.

4 Calculate the **wallpapering area** by subtracting the unpapered areas (door area + window area) from the wall area.

5 Calculate the **wallpaper to buy** by dividing the wallpapering area by the **usable yield** that is determined by the pattern repeat of your paper (see below).

Usable yield chart for wallpaper

Pattern repeat (drop)	Usable yield
0–150mm	2.5 sq. m
175–300mm	2.2 sq. m
325–450mm	2.0 sq. m
475–600mm	1.8 sq. m

HOW TO HANG WALLPAPER

Once you have chosen your starting point (see left), use a roll of paper to mark where the drops will fall around the room. Move the starting point a little if any joins are awkward.

Use a plumb line to mark a vertical line as a guide for the edge of the first drop of wallpaper. It's really important to get this right – if you start off wrong, your pattern will be uneven by the time you get to the end.

Cut a length of wallpaper, allowing enough for the drop plus about 10cm (4in) extra for trimming top and bottom. On a long, wipe-clean table, paste the paper with a wide brush, working from the centre outwards. When you reach the end of the table, gently fold the paper over, pasted side to pasted side, and continue pasting.

Hang the top section of paper, sliding it so the edge meets the line you marked and about 5cm (2in) overlaps onto the ceiling. Working from the middle, smooth down with a paperhanging brush.

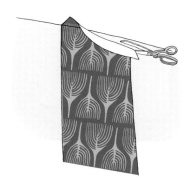

Mark the trimming line at the top with a pencil or the back of a pair of scissors. Gently peel the top edge of paper away, cut off the excess along the line and brush the edge back onto the wall. Repeat at the bottom.

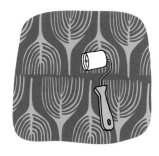

Before cutting the next drop, ensure it is long enough for you to match the pattern. Hang as before, making sure the edges join exactly. On flat papers, run a seam roller down the joins. Wipe off any excess paste with a damp sponge.

PAINT

Nothing transforms a room as quickly and easily as a fresh coat
of paint on the walls and woodwork.

ROLLER, PAD OR BRUSH?

Rollers are the most popular. They cover large areas
quickly, but may splash and can't reach into corners. They
also leave an orange-peel surface, which is unpopular with
some people. Wide brushes are a traditional choice, but
are slower and require skill to achieve a really good effect.
Pads make the paint smooth and even, but can spread it
too thinly, meaning you need more coats.

TYPES OF PAINT

- **Solvent-based paints** take longer to dry and have
  a strong smell, but they flow beautifully and dry
  smoothly; brushes need cleaning with white spirit.
  Solvent-based paint contains higher levels of VOCs
  (volatile organic compounds); according to the
  Environment Agency these can cause adverse
  health effects.
- **Water-based paints** are quick drying, with a low
  odour, but are not generally as durable as oil-based
  versions; brushes are easily cleaned with water. Water-
  based paint contains lower levels of VOCs.
- **Primer** is used to seal a bare surface and help paint to
  adhere and give a good finish.
- **Undercoat** is applied on top of primer to give 'body' to
  gloss. It comes in different colours, depending on the
  shade of topcoat to be used.
- **Emulsion** is always water-based and usually comes in
  a matt or silk (shinier) finish. Use a brush, roller or paint
  pad to apply to walls and ceilings (see above).
- **Paint for woodwork and metal** comes in a variety
  of finishes, including gloss, satin and eggshell. It may
  be oil- or water-based, and is suitable for interior and
  exterior. Non-drip and one-coat glosses are
  also available.

- **Kitchen and bathroom paints** usually have a sheen;
  they are scrubbable, can help with condensation
  problems and may include a fungicide.
- **Masonry paints** are smooth or textured, and designed
  for outdoor brickwork, stone, concrete, pebbledash
  and render.
- **Eco paints**, such as limewash, are water-based and
  made with natural ingredients. They are 'breathable',
  which is important for porous walls.
- **Specialist paints** include radiator and floor paint,
  fire-retardant and anti-burglar paint, blackboard
  paint, damp-inhibiting paint, suede-effect and
  even magnetic paint. Non-drip and one-coat glosses
  are also available.

Preparing walls

1 Give the room a good clean: vacuum or mop
floors; wipe down any woodwork with a damp
cloth; remove cobwebs and dust.

2 Put paper or plastic sheeting all around the
edges of the room.

3 Fill in any nail holes, small dents, hairline
cracks, etc., with a lightweight filler. Allow
to dry according to manufacturer's instructions
(usually 2–4 hours) then sand until smooth.

4 Clean the walls/surfaces to be painted using a
simple solution of washing-up liquid and
water. This is especially important in kitchens and
bathrooms, where different residues are commonly
built up on the walls. Finish the walls with a quick
rinse of plain water to remove any soap residue.

HOW TO PAINT YOUR WALLS

Before you start, turn off the power supply and unscrew ceiling rose covers and the faceplates of sockets and switches so that you can paint behind them.

Paint the ceiling first, starting in a corner near the window. If you can't reach the ceiling easily, use a long-handled roller or a stepladder. Use a small brush to paint a 5cm (2in) band around all the edges – you can overlap onto the walls a little, as you will 'cut in' later with your wall colour. Choose a roller sleeve with the correct fibre type and pile length for your paint and wall surface.

Going from the wet edges you have just painted, roll overlapping strokes in all directions, in bands about 60cm (23½in) wide. Start near a window so that the light on the surface shows any patches that have been missed. Reload the sleeve and apply a little further away from where you have just painted, and then blend.

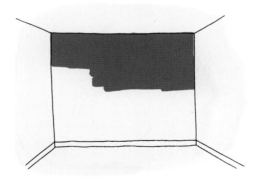

For the walls, start by cutting in at a top corner. Then, with the roller, work downwards in bands. If you are right-handed you will find it easier to work from right to left, and vice versa if you are left-handed. Finish a whole wall at a time so that areas do not dry before you blend them in, which can give a blotchy effect.

TILES

Just like wallpaper, tiles come in a fabulous variety of colours and patterns –
and can be used in all sorts of ways around your home.

Tiles can be sleek and machine-made or rustic and handmade; shiny and glazed or matt and unglazed; perfectly smooth or nicely textured; even digitally printed with your own designs. Long-lasting and hard-wearing, waterproof and easy to clean, tiles are ideal as wall finishes for bathrooms, showers and behind kitchen worktops. They are also great for hallways, conservatories, laundry and utility rooms, and, given their immense decorative potential, can sometimes work as part of a living area, too.

The visual impact of a tiled area – whether it's a whole wall or a small splashback – depends on a number of factors, including colour, pattern and texture, as well as size (from huge slabs to tiny mosaic tiles) and shape (square and rectangular are most common, but other shapes are available). What also makes a huge difference is the layout you choose – a simple grid, offset (or brick bond), herringbone, pinwheel or random, whether you use borders or a mix of different tiles, how widely they are spaced and even the colour of your grout.

A QUICK GUIDE TO TILES

▶ **Ceramic tiles:** Relatively inexpensive, these don't need sealing or polishing and are easily wiped clean.

▶ **Porcelain tiles:** Heavier and more hardwearing than ceramic tiles, these can often be used outdoors as well as indoors. Surface effects include natural stone, metals, concrete, fabric, wood and leather.

▶ **Glass tiles:** These may be clear, frosted and coloured, and have a lovely translucent appearance.

▶ **Mosaics:** Small mosaic tiles are usually supplied on a backing sheet and used for decorative effect.

▶ **Natural stone tiles:** Limestone, marble, granite and slate are all natural stone tiles. They can be porous, and often need to be sealed before use.

*Stunning Turkish-style tiles
can give your bathroom a
Mediterranean feel.*

HOW TO TILE A WALL

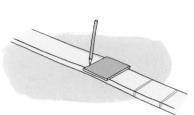

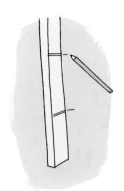

Make sure your surface is clean and dry. You can tile over existing tiles, as long as they are securely fixed. Mark up a length of wood to use as a tiling gauge, allowing for the gaps between the tiles as well. Always make sure you check your horizontal lines carefully.

'Set out' your tiled area. Find the centre of your wall and mark the position of the tiles from there. Adjust your starting point if you find you will end up cutting lots of thin slivers to fit around obstacles such as doors, windows or bathroom fittings. Ideally, you will have a border of cut tiles of the same width at the end of each row of tiles.

To support the tiles while the adhesive sets, temporarily fix battens (using part-driven masonry pins) along the wall, about half a tile height above the skirting board (depending on the setting out). Use a spirit level to check that they are horizontal. If you are tiling a large area, a vertical guide batten is also useful.

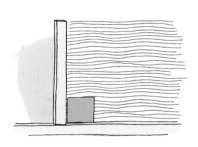

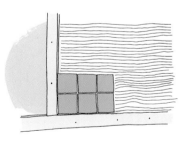

Apply the adhesive to the wall with a toothed spreader, drawing it evenly across the wall. Use enough to fix about 10 or 12 tiles. Bed the first tile into place with a slight twist, using the battens as a guide.

Add a tile spacer, then press the second tile into place, and so on, until you have completed the bottom row. Carry on spreading adhesive and adding rows until all the whole tiles are in place.

Cut tiles to fit the gaps, spread adhesive on their backs and push into place. Wait for the adhesive to set, then remove the tile spacers and battens, and tile in the space below your bottom row. Wait until this is dry and then fill the joints with grout.

OTHER WALL COVERINGS

Paint and wallpaper are not the only ways to cover a wall: with a little
imagination and ingenuity, almost any flat surface can be employed to create
an interesting decorative effect.

Mirror
A wall (or a portion of it) covered
with a sheet of mirror will reflect
light around and instantly make
the room seem bigger.

Fabric
This is a traditional-looking,
expensive technique that is
great for insulating against cold
and noise.

Leather
Unusual and expensive, leather
walls add luxurious character,
soften sounds and are even fire-
retardant. Leather develops
a patina over time.

Cork
Warm and soft to the touch,
eco-friendly, insulating and
soundproofing, cork sheets or tiles
offer many appealing qualities.

Composites and laminates
Sheets of plastic laminate or solid
composite are waterproof and
need few joins; they are a good
choice for bathrooms.

Sheet metal
Sheets of metal (steel, copper,
aluminium) can be used to create
an unusual wall installation. They
can be textured, laser-cut and
even rusty.

Polished plaster
Also known as Venetian plaster,
this old Italian technique involves
applying several thin coats of plaster
and polishing with wax. The effect
can be like marble, stone or suede.

Timber panelling
Panelling can hide uneven walls
and is a great insulator. It also has
warmth and character. Fielded
panelling gives a classic effect,
while tongue and groove is cosy
and gives a country feel.

Fixing visual problems

- ▶ If your ceiling is in poor condition, make repairs (fill cracks, sand to a smooth finish) and try covering it in a colourful wallpaper to match the rest of the room.
- ▶ Unsightly drips of paint can easily be removed. Scrape back the drip, lightly sand the area to a smooth finish and repaint the affected area. Hide stains by cleaning thoroughly, and then applying primer or undercoat. When this is dry, recoat with spare topcoat.
- ▶ Create an art panel out of wallpaper to cover a particularly rough, uneven wall surface. Buy a large picture frame or make your own frame and simply paste wallpaper to the backing board.
- ▶ Paint plain wooden fitted wardrobe or cupboard doors in the same colour as the walls to integrate them in the room. Alternatively, if the wall is wallpapered, try covering the doors in the same wallpaper.
- ▶ Don't paint walls before deciding on flooring, furniture and window treatments. It's much easier to match paint to these relatively expensive elements than vice versa.
- ▶ Remember, don't be afraid to ask for help, be it with paint colour or wallpaper. Another opinion can give you piece of mind and help you to avoid redoing costly work.

This textured wallpaper is a relatively inexpensive way to give the effect of exposed brickwork.

HOW TO PUT UP TONGUE-AND-GROOVE PANELLING

Tongue-and-groove panelling can run vertically or horizontally and is held firm by battens that run in the opposite direction. On solid walls, battens can be fixed anywhere, but on stud walls fix to the studs, or use specialist fixings. For vertical panelling, fix battens at the top and bottom and then at 40–50cm (16–20in) intervals. Either remove skirtings and architraving around doors and windows (and replace later) or put battens right up to them. Here is how to put up vertical tongue-and-groove panelling to dado height.

Measure the area to work out how much 22 x 50mm (1 x 2in) timber is needed for the battens, and how many boards you need. Trim battens to fit along each wall. Use a spirit level and mark out where the battens will go. Fix battens every 20–30cm (8–12in) using masonry pins (or screws).

Cut boards to the length required, sand and wipe clean. Work left to right from starting point. Place the first board on the wall; check it is straight. On LHS, clear of the groove, drive panel pins through the board into the battens. On RHS, drive pins through tongue into battens, one for each batten.

Slide the tongue of the next board into the groove. Using a wooden block and gentle hammer taps, ease board into position. Fix in place with pins through the tongue. Continue for the whole area. Fit the last board as you would for a corner. Use quarter round trim to neaten the edge.

At internal corners, measure the space between the last board and the corner. Cut a board slightly narrower so it is easier to fit. For the other wall do the same and butt the pieces of cut board together. Do the same for external corners. Sand the cut edges.

If you have any electrical sockets, you will need to work around these – they must not be covered up. Usually, a box extension can be added so that the socket sits just slightly proud of the panelling. It is advisable to use a qualified electrician to carry out this work.

When all the tongue-and-groove is in place, add a rail along the top and, if necessary, skirting at the bottom. Finally, apply your chosen finish – varnish, wood stain or paint.

CEILINGS

Although they may be percieved as large, blank surfaces, ceilings do contribute to the decorative effect of a room. This is especially true in period properties when ceilings were adorned with elaborate plasterwork.

DIFFERENT TREATMENTS

In modern homes, the majority of ceilings are painted in a matt white paint. White does reflect more light than any colour and, consequently, it promotes height. If a room has a disproportionately high ceiling, use a subtle colour to lower and improve the sense of proportion and atmosphere. Conversely, to create the illusion that your ceiling is higher, use the same paint colour on the woodwork, walls, cornice or coving, with a white that is sympathetic to the wall colour on the ceiling – this will make the walls appear taller. For a truly dramatic effect, use the same colour on the ceiling, so that you are less aware of where the walls end and the ceiling begins.

On a similar theme, paint the ceiling the same colour as the walls, but then pick out any period features, such as ceiling roses, cornices or picture rails in a lighter shade.

In bedrooms, where ceilings are viewed as much as other parts of the room, you could choose a shade (lighter or darker) that contrasts with the main colour, or apply some of the above suggestions. And instead of a feature wall, try wallpapering the ceiling!

PERIOD FEATURES

Classically inspired plasterwork for ceilings (found in Georgian and Victorian properties) includes ceiling roses, moulded cornices at the junction between the wall and ceiling, and decorative friezes below the cornices. In the Victorian period, especially after the introduction of mass-produced mouldings, plasterwork became even more ornate. If you have these features in your home, it is definitely worth repairing or restoring them to enhance the character of your home. And if original features have been removed, you can buy suitable replacements, made from fibrous plaster.

PANELLED OR BEAMED CEILINGS

Originally, ceilings were simply the underside of the roof covering, or the bottom of the floorboards in the

room above. Plaster was sometimes used to finish the underside, leaving the beams exposed. This type of ceiling is a common feature of many cottages. Generally, if the ceiling is in good condition it's best to leave the beams and just paint the plaster. Beamed ceilings have been reproduced in various properties, for instance, in mock-Tudor houses. In such cases you might want to treat the beams and plaster as one and paint in the same colour.

MATCHBOARDING

This is a form of tongue-and-groove cladding often used on ceilings. It can completely cover a surface or can be fitted between beams, and can be painted or sealed. Matchboarding can be useful for covering a ceiling that is in poor repair.

WINDOWS

Windows are designed to let in light and air, whilst minimising heat loss;
at the same time they are important architectural features,
which will enhance any interior design scheme.

The way you incorporate windows into your design scheme will depend not only on your personal taste and style of the room, but also the number of windows you have – whether you have a Georgian sash window, a large bay window, a pair of plain casement windows, or large French windows. Nonetheless, unless you have a very unsightly window that you want to hide or partially obscure, avoid anything that covers windows unnecessarily, so they let in as much light as possible. If you have original stained glass windows, it is a shame to cover them; in a hallway they are very welcoming.

Dealing with difficult shapes, such as arched windows, can be problematic. Here, you could use a café-style curtain or a blind halfway up, leaving the arch free. Otherwise hang curtains or blinds high above the arch.

For a particularly beautiful window (and a lovely arched window), it might be advisable not to put up any curtains or blinds, that is, if privacy is not an issue and the window overlooks a wonderful view. Conversely, if you have a window that has a particularly unattractive view, you might want to replace clear glass with opaque glass. No longer is frosted glass the only option: you can re-glaze with sandblasted glass, perhaps with a clear edge or decorative motif. An inexpensive option is glass spray frosting or sticky-back opaque window plastic.

There are many imaginative ways of decorating windows, including shutters (plantation and antique panelled shutters), lattice-work screens and using stencilling to look like etched glass. The latter can provide privacy as well as a lovely finish for a plain, dull window – you can even fit shelves across an uninteresting window.

Always remember that the inside treatment will be seen from the outside – during the day, and especially in the evening when the lights are on. Unlined curtains or blinds can work in certain situations, but if the colour or pattern is really vivid and bold, make sure you are happy about the view from outside. Take account of all the window treatments, which will be seen together.

Before you go to great expense, think about the type, size and number of windows you have and how you plan to decorate the rest of the room. Opposite are some examples of common types of windows.

A roller blind has been positioned high above this large, unusual-shaped window to show it off to its best advantage.

TYPES OF WINDOWS

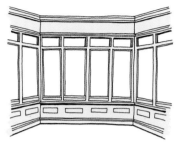

Bay window

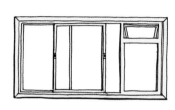

Horizontal window

Casement window

French windows

Georgian sash window

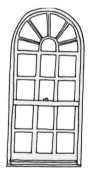

Arched window

Skylight

Dormer window

WINDOW TREATMENTS

Practical as well as pretty, curtains, blinds and shutters are
an important feature in every room.

Window treatments are often necessary for privacy,
and may help with insulation, soundproofing and even
security, but they are much more than just a functional
addition to a room. A well-designed set of curtains, blinds
or shutters will complement the overall design scheme –
and can correct a badly proportioned window, disguise
an unattractive view, filter bright light, provide a visual link
between inside and out and, in general, give the space a
satisfyingly 'finished' feel.

Before you start, establish your priorities. If your
window treatment is there purely to keep out prying eyes,
an inexpensive blind or muslin café curtain may be just
the thing – or even stick-on window film, easy to apply,
cheap and available in a variety of different patterns. Save
money where possible, because professionally made,
lavish window treatments can be costly (though they
should last a long time). For light control, blinds and
louvred shutters are better than traditional curtains, while
layered window treatments – curtains as well as shutters,

perhaps – can give you more options. Consider whether
you would like 'extras' such as pelmets, tie-backs and
the like – they may give a more sophisticated look, but
costs can soon mount up. And make sure each window
treatment really suits the space: we are talking durable
shutters or hard-wearing fabric curtains in children's
rooms and sitting rooms, splashproof blinds in kitchens
and bathrooms and silk curtains in bedrooms, for
example. Once you have made the basic decisions, there
are a wonderful variety of styles from which to choose.

INSTANT WINDOW TREATMENTS

Lace panel
A pretty way to provide privacy. Use vintage lace for an interesting effect. Muslin is a plainer, but value-for-money alternative.

Sari fabric
Gorgeous colours and patterns, sometimes including metallic thread, make this a very decorative option for dressing windows.

Blanket
A lightweight blanket will drape well over a large window or can be turned into a blind. There are plain and patterned options.

Lightweight rug
Punch eyelet holes in the rug and thread over a sturdy pole, and you have instant pattern and colour.

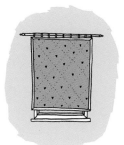

Small quilt / bedcover / throw
Think laterally and use bed coverings as window treatments. Large and already hemmed, they can be just the ticket.

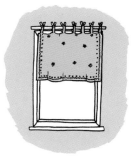

Tablecloth
There are all sorts of options, from embroidered to gingham to plain. Inexpensive, quick and easy.

CURTAINS

Choosing and fitting curtains is more than a matter of finding beautiful fabric that will enhance your room – you'll need to consider their length and style, and how they will be hung, too.

FABRIC

Curtains can be made from practically any fabric. The heavier the fabric, the better it will hold a fold, although very heavy fabrics will be too bulky for small windows (and require a sturdy track or pole). Light fabrics can look floppy unless they are lined, and will let daylight through.

LININGS

Linings are essential on all but sheers to help curtains hang neatly and protect them from fading, dirt and condensation. Blackout linings are ideal in a bedroom that gets sun in the mornings, while thermal linings can be as effective as double-glazing.

LENGTH AND WIDTH

To let maximum light into the room, fit a pole or track that overhangs far enough each side to allow the curtains to be drawn right away from the window – bearing in mind that full, thick curtains need more 'stack back' space than light, thin ones. Floor-length curtains are generally better than sill-length, although shorter curtains may suit the space better when radiators or window seats are in the way.

HEADINGS AND HANGINGS

The way in which a curtain hangs is determined by its heading, often created by a tape sewn onto the back of the curtain and pulled to form gathers or pleats. For a less formal look, options include tab- and tie-tops (often found on ready-made curtains, but fiddly to draw), a deep hem that slides over a pole, large eyelets, clips (magnetic ones are easy to use) or even just some hooks.

POLES, TRACKS, WIRES AND RODS

The most straightforward way to hang curtains is from a pole, though you need some clearance above and below for it to look right. Finished with plain or decorative finials, poles are designed to be on show. Tracks, on the other hand, are more subtle. Made from plastic (inexpensive)

Extra-long curtains give a sumptuous look.

or metal (smart), they can be mounted either on the wall or ceiling; they also bend around bay windows. Double tracks allow you to hang both sheers or nets and thicker curtains neatly. On narrow windows or dormers, portiere (swing-arm) rods are an alternative to fixed poles, while for a modern effect you could use tension wire, fixed taut within the window opening.

HOW TO MEASURE UP CURTAINS

Whatever style of curtain you plan to make, accurate measuring is vital for a professional finish. Use a metre rule, a folding ruler or a rectractable metal tape measure and enlist a helper if the window is large.

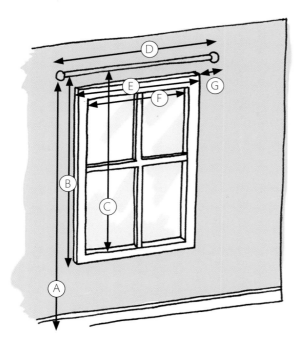

A Bottom of pole, track or rod to floor.

B Bottom of pole, track or rod to bottom of window frame

C Bottom of pole, track or rod to sill

D Length of pole, track or rod

E Width of window frame from outside edge to outside edge

F Width of window recess

G Stacking space (also on left-hand side of window)

GLOSSARY OF MEASURING TERMS

Fabric width – the purchased width of the fabric.

Selvedge – the tightly woven edge of the fabric. This reacts differently to the main fabric to stitching and washing and so should be cut off unless you are working with velvet.

Cut width – the width of the fabric after the selvedge has been removed.

Finished width – the full width of the area that the completed curtain is intended to cover, including the stacking space (see opposite).

Widths – multiples of the cut width of the fabric. With the exception of a very small window, you will probably need to join more than one width of fabric to make up a curtain.

Finished drop or drop – the full length of the area that the completed curtain is intended to cover.

Cut drop – the finished drop plus hem, heading and pattern repeat allowances. This is the measurement to cut before assembling the curtain.

Fixture – the mechanism from which a curtain is hung, including tracks, poles and rods. The fixture can be mounted on the wall over the window frame, on the frame or inside the recess depending on the style of the window (see page 63) and style of curtain.

CHOOSING CURTAINS

Traditional or contemporary, curtains can add pattern, colour and texture to
any room. They can be bright and bold or subdued and understated, and on
a practical level they can provide you with privacy, darkness and warmth.

Think about the overall style of your room – formal or informal. If the room is already decorated, take account of the other furnishings in the room. If you are going for a period look, then you might want to choose a traditional style with a patterned fabric. If you want a modern look, then choose from simple designs with plain-coloured fabrics and eyelet headings.

TYPES OF CURTAINS AND HEADINGS

▸ **Curtain headings** determine the shape and size of the pleats and gathers, and pull in the fabric to fit the required width.

▸ **Pencil pleated curtains** have thin, evenly spaced pleats, running continuously across the curtain. This style of heading can be used in traditional and contemporary settings, and suits full-length curtains.

▸ **French (or pinch) pleats** usually consist of three pleats with flat areas in between each group of pleats. Like pencil pleats, they suit full-length curtains, but make for a more formal look.

▸ **Simple, narrow, gathered heading tape** is used on many different types of curtains, lined and unlined. Curtains with this type of heading are often used behind a pelmet or valance.

▸ **Curtains with heading tape** can be used on a track (using plastic curtain hooks) or a pole (with hooks and wooden or metal curtain rings).

▸ **Curtains with eyelet headings** (usually metal, of varying diameters) produce a softer, wider fold, and have to be used with a pole. Choose this type of curtain for a modern scheme.

▸ **Tab (or tie) headings** produce a fairly flat curtain, depending on the amount of tabs; best used in contemporary designs.

▸ **Curtains with a case heading** simply have a tube at the top of the curtain. They will not slide easily so are usually used for lightweight curtains, such as sheers, that do not need to be drawn.

Curtain fixtures

▸ When choosing a fixture (track, pole or wire) for your curtains, decide whether you want it concealed or visible, period or contemporary, pull cords or none. Consider the style of your room and the type of curtains/fabric you want.

▸ Tracks for curtains come in a wide variety of materials, including PVC, aluminium and steel. Choose your track depending on the weight of your curtains, and whether it needs to be flexible. PVC is inexpensive and suitable for light- and medium-weight fabric; aluminium or steel is more expensive, but is suitable for heavy curtains. Both plastic and metal curtain tracks can be bent, but some are stronger than others. In addition, you can buy corded or un-corded tracks.

▸ Poles are designed to be visible, and come in a variety of materials, sizes and finishes. Unsealed poles can be painted or stained; you can make your own or even use an antique pole. You will need matching supports and, unless the pole fits inside a window recess, finials.

▸ Curtain wire in stainless steel, which can be bought complete with fittings, is another contemporary choice for lightweight curtains.

▸ Pelmets and valances fit over curtain tracks. Pelmets can be made from wood or other stiff materials; they can be painted or covered with fabric. Valances are made by pleating or gathering fabric so that it fits across the top of the curtains, but they are not mounted onto a board.

▸ Tie-backs wrap around curtains and hold them out of the way. Attached to the wall using a hook, they can be simple or decorative. Hold-backs are made from wood or metal and are fixed to the wall; the curtain is hooked behind them.

HOW TO HANG
PENCIL PLEAT CURTAINS

First, adjust the curtains to the width they will be when they are closed. To do this, knot the loose cords in the heading tape at one end. Pull the cords at the opposite end to gather up the fabric into even pleats until the curtain is the width required. Knot the free cords, but not too tightly, and never cut the ends. Remember they will need to be loosened/undone when you clean the curtains.

Now insert the hooks into the heading tape. There is usually a choice of two or three levels. For tracks, slot the hooks into the lower row so that the track is covered as above. For poles, use the top row so that the curtain hangs below the pole. Place one hook at each end of the curtain and space the others about 8cm (3in) apart. Use the same amount of hooks in each curtain, and check that you have the same amount of gliders (track) or rings.

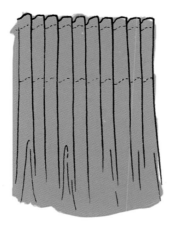

Make sure that the pleats are neat and evenly spaced, depending how full the curtains are. Lastly, attach each hook to a glider or ring. Curtains do need time to settle; it may take a little while for them to fall correctly.

BLINDS

Perfect for smaller rooms where grand window treatments are not quite so appropriate, blinds are also great for modern spaces where you want an understated style – and, because they need far less fabric, they tend to be a lot cheaper than curtains. If you are handy with a sewing machine, you may even be able to make them yourself.

▶ **Roller blinds** are the most basic style, while roll-up blinds, tied with tape or ribbon, have a pretty yet still simple look.

▶ **Roman blinds**, which pull up into soft, wide pleats, are smart and versatile, suiting almost every room. When choosing fabric, opt for something that is mid-weight and not too textured, as blinds need to roll or fold easily against themselves. But there is nothing to stop you combining more than one colour or pattern, in the form of smart, contrast borders down the sides or along the bottom of the blind. And sometimes it's a good idea to combine a plain and a sheer fabric, to allow light through at the top of the window while giving privacy beneath.

▶ **Plain blinds** can be boosted with a good-looking pull (think leather, glass, raffia, stone or rope) or trim (such as ribbon, pom-poms, ric-rac, stitching, fringing, shells or buttons). If you want a dressier look, add curtains as well.

▶ **Venetian blinds** in wood, metal or plastic give a modern look and are a good way to add privacy and let in light at the same time.

Roller blinds are simple and work well in kitchens.

Roman blinds are always smart and are a neat way to cover a bay window.

CHOOSING BLINDS

When they are pulled down, blinds hang flat against the window, so any
inaccuracies in measure will be obvious. Measure carefully using a tape
measure or folding ruler and ask a friend to help if needs be.

As with choosing curtains, deciding on the type of blind
and fabric you want will be determined to some extent by
the type of window and, of course, the style of the room.
However, blinds are generally more suited to modern
spaces where a simple window treatment works well. With
their clean lines, they allow all types of windows to remain
uncluttered, especially small and difficult windows, such as
skylights. For a particularly large window, it is sometimes
best to use two or three separate blinds.

Like curtains, blinds can be functional, providing you
with privacy, darkness and warmth. Venetian blinds, in
particular, are an ideal choice if you require privacy in,

say, a bathroom. Roman blinds lined with blackout
fabric offer complete darkness in a bedroom, and in
living rooms they can be interlined to help insulation. In
kitchens, a roller blind made from waterproofed fabric is
a good choice.

While curtains are an eye-catching use of fabric,
blinds can also provide impact. A bold, striped Roman
blind in an otherwise plain scheme can be very striking.
And white, wooden Venetian blinds offer a stylish
solution to a bay window, as well as giving a room a
wonderful mellow light.

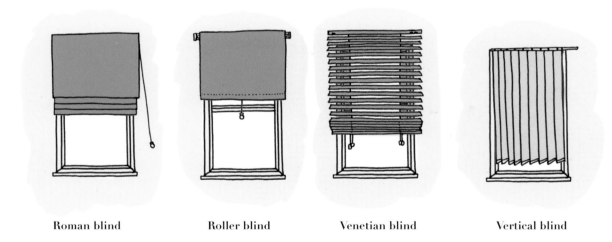

Roman blind   **Roller blind**   **Venetian blind**   **Vertical blind**

MAKING A ROMAN BLIND

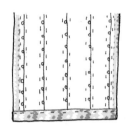

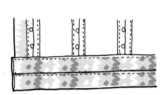

Measure the height and width of your window, adding 15cm (6in) for top and bottom hems, and 7.5cm (3in) for the side hems of the blind fabric. Join any necessary widths (of fabric and lining), matching any pattern. Cut out the fabric and lining, making the lining 5cm (2in) narrower. With right sides together, using a 1.5cm ($^5/_8$in) seam allowance, sew the lining to the fabric along each side and the top. Turn inside out and press flat.

Turn up the bottom edge of the blind 1cm ($^3/_8$in) to the lining side, and then a further 10cm (4in). Press and then pin close to the folded edge. Next, pin the blind tape in place, making sure that the rings or loops run parallel in horizontal lines. Start at the two side seams, and then at evenly spaced intervals of 15–20cm (6–8in); the closer the lengths of tape, the more tailored the folds. At the bottom the tape should just reach the fold of the hem.

When all the tapes are pinned in place, machine stitch the lower hem on the folded edge. Next make a parallel line about 4cm (1½in) below this, in order to make a casing for the batten. Machine stitch the tape in place along both edges. At the bottom, stop at the hem.

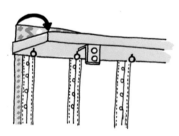

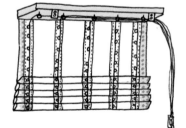

Attach brackets to the batten with screws. At the top of the blind, fold over 2.5cm (1in), press and stitch in place. Using tacks (or staples) every 10cm (4in), attach the blind to the batten. Now fix screw eyes into the underside of the batten to line up with each of the tapes. Slide in the batten and slipstitch the ends to close the casing.

At the side of the window that is most convenient, fit a cleat hook. Thread nylon cord through the bottom loop/ring of the side tape (on the opposite side to the cleat hook), across the top through the screw eyes and down the length of the blind at the side. Make sure that the cord is secured with a strong knot at the bottom. Repeat for each line of tape.

Fix your blind in place. Before drawing up the blind, make sure that all the cords are at an even tension and then tie the ends together. Next, gently pull up the blind and ease the cords around the cleat hook. Smooth the pleats into place evenly and leave drawn up for a day so that the folds will form automatically.

SHUTTERS

Good-looking in an unfussy kind of way, shutters suit both old and new properties. They are expensive but, on the plus side, they are good at blocking out sound and light, and can even provide extra security.

The plainest shutters feature a timber frame and solid centre panel (a local joiner should be able to make them for you). Louvred versions (from specialist shutter companies) offer privacy while also controlling the light. Both types can be left as natural wood, or painted whatever colour you like. They can be made as a pair, bi- or tri-fold or in other groupings, either full- or half-height, or one set above another, and fitted within a reveal or to fold back against the walls. For a striking and modern effect, opt for shutters made from opaque or coloured acrylic. Elegant, with a modern edge, they are translucent, so may need to be combined with blinds for night-time privacy.

Shutters fold back completely to let the maximum amount of light into a room.

LIGHTING

As well as making interiors seem bigger, brighter and fresher, clever lighting can give 'va-va voom' to the simplest of decorative schemes.

When a room seems boring, bland and lifeless, it is often the lighting that is to blame. A well-designed lighting scheme, on the other hand, emphasises good points, highlights colour, texture and shapes, and disguises problem areas. On a practical note, we need adequate lighting to help us carry out day-to-day activities easily and safely. And on a psychological level, light sends out signals of warmth, welcome and vitality – reinforcing a sense of comfort and security.

In many ways, the best lighting is invisible: in other words, you don't notice the fitting itself, just the fact that it illuminates efficiently and beautifully. Ideally, it is best to design a lighting scheme at the earliest stages, when you are planning how a room will be used and where furniture will be placed. Think about how you will live in the space,

and then ask yourself where you will need light, how much you will require at different times of day and night, which areas you want to highlight and what effects you wish to create. Only then can you wire in lights or install plug sockets exactly where you'll need them.

There are four main types: overall general light; bright light for working by; accent lighting for special features; and atmosphere lighting, which sets the mood. Try to design a scheme that employs several of these types, using light from more than one direction – think of it as painting with light, creating washes and filling in with highlights and lowlights.

These metallic ceiling lights make a dramatic statement by themselves, but here they also reflect the vibrant colours used in the design scheme.

TYPES OF LIGHTING

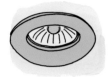

Downlights
Either set into the ceiling or mounted onto it, downlights may be fixed or adjustable. A good source of general lighting.

Strip lights
Functional and often energy saving, these simple lights are useful for working areas such as kitchens or utility rooms.

Tracks
A row of spotlights can be attached to a straight or curved track when it is not possible to recess lights in the ceiling.

Spotlight
Individual spotlights are ideal for highlighting special features. In work areas or dark corners, clip-on versions are practical.

Uplighters
Fixed at eye level or higher, uplighters bounce light onto the ceiling and can help make a room seem bigger.

Wall lights
By diffusing a soft glow around the room, wall lights are an excellent source of general lighting.

Floor lamps
These tall fittings are useful for adding light to corners of rooms, and perfect next to a reading chair.

Table lamps
Often inexpensive, table lamps are a versatile way to add light in dark corners and make a room more welcoming.

Shelf lights
Fitted under a shelf, these lights illuminate the display or work area below. There are also versions for glass shelves.

Desk lights
A hinged-arm, Anglepoise-style lamp is ideal for illuminating your work. The more adjustable it is, the better.

Pendants
Often hung in the centre of a room, pendant lights range from decorative chandeliers to simple modern fittings.

Outdoor lights
Security lights, spotlights, floodlights, party lights and decorative solar fittings can transform an outside space.

LIGHTING ROOM BY ROOM

Make sure that every room in your home is illuminated beautifully, with bright, clear light for practical tasks, highlights for special features and a warm, welcoming glow for ambience and comfort.

LIVING ROOMS

Ideally, install a flexible range of options, from bright reading lights beside seating to softer, ambient lights for relaxing and entertaining. You could also highlight shelving, pictures or a coffee table. Don't forget fires and candlelight, for a romantic, soft glow.

DINING ROOMS

A pendant hung over a dining table creates an intimate atmosphere (but make sure it is hung above eye level). Fix wall lights a little lower than eye level – it works better when you are sitting down.

KITCHENS

Adjustable spotlights, on tracks or in the ceiling, are practical for general light. Mount bright lights (tubes or downlights) beneath wall cabinets to illuminate worksurfaces.

BATHROOMS

Combine directional task lights – ceiling downlights or tracks – with softer lights, such as LED wall washers. Because shiny surfaces reflect light, you may need fewer light sources or lower wattages than you expect. Only use fittings designed to be safe in wet and steamy conditions.

BEDROOMS

Here subtle, flattering lighting is needed, although a good light for mirrors is essential. Wall-mounted lights free up space on a bedside table.

HALLS AND STAIRS

Lighting should be warm and welcoming. Staircases must be brightly and evenly lit, with a switch at the top and bottom.

QUICK TRICKS WITH LIGHTING

▶ Change the bulb – a brighter or softer one may work better; or try a more mellow tone.

▶ Change the shade – a new shape or colour may make all the difference. But do choose a replacement shade that's in proportion with both the light fitting and the room as a whole.

▶ Use dimmer switches wherever possible and gain complete control over your level of lighting.

▶ Add a lamp in a dark corner: table lamps, floor lamps and even clip-on spotlights can all work wonders.

▶ Extend the cord of a central pendant – you can then change its position by hooking it from a cup hook screwed into the ceiling.

▶ Add fairy lights around mantelpieces or over bedheads for a pretty twinkle.

▶ For extra light outdoors, try solar-powered lanterns or stake lights. They are instant, easy, inexpensive and eco-conscious, too.

▶ Turn your lights right down and light a few candles. They look particularly effective grouped together, and you just can't beat their warm, flickering glow.

Mixing traditional furniture and modern floor lights can work extremely well.

Wall lights placed above the bed create more space on bedside tables.

Concealed, colour-change lighting adds interest to this living room design.

Make the most of natural light

▶ Clean the windows.

▶ Remove ornaments from window sills.

▶ Make sure curtains and blinds don't hang in front of windows when open.

▶ Hang a large mirror opposite a window.

▶ Replace a solid door with a glazed one.

▶ Consider enlarging or adding windows, or installing a skylight or sun pipe.

FITTINGS AND FUNCTIONS

When selecting light fittings, take account of the quality of light that is
needed for the task and function of the room.

CEILING LIGHTS

Ceiling lights are fixed to the ceiling and provide good
illumination for the whole room. The downside is that it is
difficult to control glare and create shadow and contrast.
Installing a dimmer switch can help to reduce glare. In
halls, staircases and landings, where you need to be able
to see where you are going, overhead lighting is effective.

PENDANT LIGHTS

Hanging from the ceiling, pendant light fittings can be
used for atmosphere and general lighting. As with most
fittings, the quality of the light depends on the type of
bulbs and shades used. A pendant with a translucent
shade that encloses the bulb, such as a glass globe, will
disperse light around the room. Light can be directed
downwards with a shade that is open at the bottom. This
type of shade looks good over a table; it also helps if the
pendant is adjustable so that the light can be brought
closer to the table when required.

DOWNLIGHTERS

As the name suggests, downlighters spread a beam of light
from the ceiling to the floor. The width of the beam varies

according to the fitting. They can be surface-mounted,
recessed or semi-recessed into the ceiling. Track lighting
– a form of downlighting – offers flexibility as it allows
you to move fittings anywhere along the track. Downlight
fittings provide general, mood and task lighting. They are
useful for rooms with low ceilings.

UPLIGHTERS

With uplighters you get soft, general illumination without
glare; the light bounces off the ceiling, which acts as a
reflector. Uplighters are relatively inexpensive and come
in various forms, from semi-circular wall sconces to tall
floor lamps with cone-shaped shades. Both the shape of
the fitting or shade and the type of bulb used will have
an effect on the area that is lit. Use them to highlight
attractive features, such as period plasterwork.

DIMMERS

Dimmer switches allow you to adjust the light, according
to the atmosphere you wish to create – turn high for
a cool bright light for reading, or low for a subdued,
soft glow for listening to music. Dimmers are not very
expensive so it's a good idea to fit them wherever possible
– they create fantastic effects at the flick of a switch.

LIGHT BULBS

▸ **Energy-efficient (EE) bulbs** have now replaced
  tungsten bulbs and have become the norm; they are
  available in a wide range of shapes and sizes to fit most
  lamps and light fixtures.
▸ **Halogen bulbs** are 10–15% more efficient and
  longer-lasting than the old tungsten bulbs, though less
  eco-friendly than EE bulbs. Compact in size, they can
  be used with dimmer switches.
▸ **LEDs (light emitting diodes)** are the most eco-friendly
  and long-lasting, but are not very bright, so are best
  used for accent lighting and children's bedrooms.
▸ **Fibre-optic lights** in a variety of colours can be used to
  create mood and atmosphere.

HOW TO COVER A LAMPSHADE

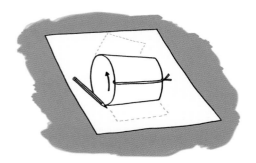

To make a template, tie a length of wool around the shade. Place on its side on some newspaper with the wool touching the paper. Mark this point and roll the shade and the wool across the paper, marking its path top and bottom until you have gone through 360°. Add 1cm (⅜in) around your finished shape and cut out.

Place the template on the right side of the fabric and cut out. With the fabric right side down, turn up 1cm (⅜in) along both long edges and one short edge and press. Place the fabric over the shade, lining up the seams.

Using spray fabric adhesive, and following the manufacturer's instructions, spray along the unpressed edge and then smooth the pressed edge over the top for a neat finish. Spray the seam allowance along top and bottom edges of the fabric and carefully fold down over the shade. Then use fire-retardant spray over the entire shade according to the manufacturer's instructions.

HEATING

Always consider heating and insulation as soon as you move into a new home, or if you decide to update your existing one – comfort and economy should be considered as well as appearance.

Heating is vital in any home, but it can be unobtrusive, if you so choose. Nonetheless, it is advisable to plan your heating in relation to any other interior changes you are making. The same goes for insulation, as some decorative finishes and features can themselves provide you with insulation. Heating systems are also expensive so you will need to budget carefully, and because they are often complicated and disruptive, it is wise to have it installed by specialists. Pipework should be incorporated into the structure of the house and this is a skilled job.

Ideally, heating and insulation should keep you warm in cold weather and cool in warm weather. Central heating is the ideal system in most situations, but the type you choose – electric, gas, oil, under-floor or radiators – is dependant on the kind of house you live in, its location, what level of insulation it has and what fuels are available at what price. Generally, it is worth spending more initially on a system in order to use fuel more efficiently.

In Britain, as elsewhere, we are experiencing climate change, but generally, air conditioning is only really needed in hot climates.

INSULATION

It is crucial to have good insulation – it keeps heat from escaping through walls, floors, roofs, windows and doors. It also keeps the house cool in warmer periods. The better insulated the home, the more efficient the heating system will be. Insulation reduces energy consumption and minimises environmental damage. A simple way of insulating the home is to lay carpet and hang interlined curtains. Other forms include: double glazing; draught-stripping windows and doors; lagging lofts, hot-water pipes, cylinders and storage cisterns.

RADIATORS

The siting of radiators is as important as the style you choose. It's best to take advice from specialists. But

remember that radiators should not be blocked by furniture or heavy curtains. Today, there is a huge choice of radiators available, from standard, steel-panel radiators to more expensive cast-iron and aluminium ones of different shapes and sizes with sculptural qualities.

FIREPLACES

A fireplace is traditionally the focal point of a room. In period properties the right choice of fireplace can bring the whole interior together. In the post-war period, fireplaces were often boxed in or removed – it is worth restoring an original fireplace or putting in a replacement. Choose a reproduction fireplace that is appropriate for the style of your home or room. If you plan to have an open fire, make sure that the chimney is sound and have the chimney swept before installing the fireplace.

TYPES OF RADIATOR

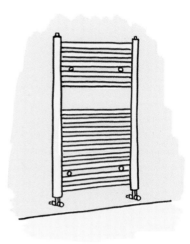

Heated towel rail
Very useful in bathrooms both for heating and for drying off towels after bathing. They come in a wide range of sizes and materials.

Vertical radiator
Great for small spaces as they are taller than they are wide; there is less opportunity for them to be covered and more surface area means a greater heat output.

A very elegant option, and although they are more expensive than other types of radiators, they retain heat efficiently, they are extremely reliable and require little maintenance.

Panel radiator
Inexpensive and widely available, panel radiators come as single- or double-panel versions. Double-panel radiators produce more heat, but single panels take up less room and can be better for small spaces.

TYPES OF HEATING

Having a thorough understanding of what works where is very important
if you want to get the best out of your heating system.

At a basic level a central heating system converts fuel (usually gas or electricity, and to a lesser extent oil) to heat in a boiler, and then distributes it to different parts of the house. There are two main types of heat: radiant and convected. Radiant heat comes directly from the hot surface of the appliance, whereas convected heat is in the form of warm air, for instance, underfloor heating. Many people like to have a combination of both.

Previously, gas boilers were large and bulky, but today they are a great deal more compact, and far more efficient; they can be wall-mounted or freestanding. Increasingly, combination condensing boilers, which heat water directly from the mains when there is a demand for hot water, are being fitted – thus doing away with the need for hot-water cylinders or cold-water cisterns. If you have an old boiler it is worth changing it for an energy-efficient, updated design.

In any heating system, thermostatic control is crucial; you do not want to overheat rooms that are not being used, for example, and waste fuel. Often the hallway is a recommended place for the thermostat, but you can fit individual ones on each radiator.

ROOM HEATERS

▶ **An open fire** using coal, smokeless fuel or wood (depending on where you live), is a real pleasure on a damp and gloomy winter evening. If the fireplace has been removed and you are left with a blank chimney breast, you can simply fit a freestanding fire or log basket in the recess. Alternatively, a modern fireplace, with a reflective surround, can be inserted in a plastered chimney breast above floor level.

▶ **Wood-burning stoves** can look good in both period and contemporary homes and suit all types of rooms. They are more efficient than open fires: far less hot air is lost through the flue of a stove, and the heat output is generally higher, too. Stoves combine the functions of providing heat – sometimes also heating water – as well as a glowing focal point. There are many types available: restored antique stoves and modern stoves in many different sizes. They can be freestanding (as long as the flue can be accommodated through the roof or an outside wall) or fitted into a chimney breast, with or without a fire surround. **Note:** there are stringent safety precautions for flue maintenance and installation.

▶ **Gas fires** are not as inviting as open fires and wood-burning stoves but they can be switched on easily and do not require attention. They produce either radiant or convected heat, or a combination of both. Coal- or log-effect gas fires look good in different styles of fireplace, but they are not very efficient – just like open fires, the heat is lost up the chimney.

▶ **Separate heaters** – electric fires, fan heaters, plug-in radiators – are efficient but can be expensive to run. They can be used in conjunction with central heating systems. They are useful for rooms that are infrequently used, or when central heating is not possible. In addition, they can be used to offset severe cold weather, and also in an emergency if the central heating system breaks down. If there is adequate ventilation in the room, portable gas heaters are another option, but are quite bulky and can cause condensation.

TYPES OF FIREPLACE

Open fire with chimney
Open fires continue to be popular and provide a glowing focal point for a room during the winter months. Make sure you have a fireguard and maintain the fireplace properly.

Wood-burning stove
More efficient than open fires – up to 87 per cent compared to 25 per cent for an open fire – wood-burning stoves do still need a constant stock of seasoned wood for burning.

Inset gas or electric fire
Gas fires can be installed in existing chimney breasts or using a flue box, a flue liner and false chimney breast. Electric fires can be sited anywhere there is a plug socket nearby.

Wall-hung fire
Wall-hung fires can provide a focal point in a room where there is no existing fireplace, or in a contemporary scheme. They are also energy-efficient and space-saving.

COLOUR

Designers have a useful tool to help them with their schemes. A colour
wheel will give you the colour confidence to fill your home with an inspired
choice of hues.

Colour can be mellow and muted or thrilling and dynamic
– and it affects us in a powerful way. Our strong response
to colour stems from millions of years of evolution, in
which different hues served as vital indicators of danger
or safety: poisonous yellow berries or lush green fields,
for example.

Colour can uplift or depress us, and can even produce
a physical reaction: bright red induces a rapid heartbeat
and is an appetite stimulant, while soft blue causes the
body to produce calming chemicals. Colour is also
symbolic: red for anger, white for purity, yellow for
cowardice, and so on. And, of course, we each have our

own feelings about colour, so that one person's exciting,
energising room is another's nightmare of brash,
clashing shades. Colour is often the key to the overall
look and feel of a room: it is an incredibly versatile,
effective and satisfying tool. And, of course, our colour
choices are as individual as we are, which is exactly why
colour can be so creative.

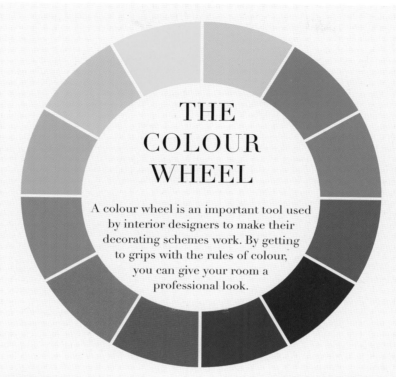

THE COLOUR WHEEL

A colour wheel is an important tool used by interior designers to make their decorating schemes work. By getting to grips with the rules of colour, you can give your room a professional look.

PRIMARY COLOURS

All colours are derived from different combinations of the three primary colours: red, yellow and blue.

SECONDARY COLOURS

Equal amounts of any two of the primary colours creates a secondary colour:

red + yellow = orange
yellow + blue = green
blue + red = violet (purple)

TERTIARY COLOURS

If you mix equal quantities of a primary and a secondary colour this creates a tertiary colour: red-orange, blue-green, etc.

If these colours are plotted in a circle you can see how the colour wheel builds up. A full colour wheel contains many different colour combinations and also includes all the different tones of each colour.

WARM AND COOL COLOURS

On the left hand side of the colour wheel the colours are 'warm' or 'hot', while the ones on the right are 'cool' or 'cold'. This is useful when you want to create a mood in a particular room or need to make your space cosier or lighter.

ACCENT COLOURS

These are used in quite small quantities to lift or to add impact to a colour scheme and should be in a complementary colour – one that appears directly opposite on the colour wheel. Keep most of your room in shades of just one colour; choose a number of items in a harmonious colour; and include just a few objects in an accent colour.

CLASHING COLOURS

In the home, if used carefully, clashing colours can look fantastic. If they are of equal tonal strength, you can mix them together, but if one is paler or weaker than the rest it will get lost in the overall scheme.

VERSATILE NEUTRALS

Neutral colours are the little black dresses of interior design: easy
to use, versatile and always good-looking.

Understated, calm and inviting, neutral colours are timelessly fashionable and eternally appealing. They link rooms harmoniously, look good in small or large spaces and provide the perfect backdrop for works of art or collections.

There is only one drawback. Let's face it: neutrals can be a little dull. Even though they come in an almost infinite range of colours, from the subtlest off-white to sandy tones, greys to taupes, the nicest neutral can be boring if it is used everywhere. The solution? Easy – darker tones for woodwork and lighter ones for walls or, if you have features such as cornices and dadoes, you can paint lighter shades above the divisions and darker ones below.

Another mistake with neutrals is to use different hues that are all the same tone – in other words, slightly different colours but the same degree of lightness or darkness. You can end up with a horrible clash. This may sound complicated, but it isn't rocket science. To select a nice variation of tones, simply pick up a colour chart and go up or down (dark to light) within the same colour family, rather than working across from colour to colour.

A PERFECT FINISH

Finally, the plainer the colours, the more important texture becomes. So, when using neutrals, it's important to choose your finishes as carefully as you do the colours. Not only do they create visual interest, they can even affect the look of the paints themselves. A high gloss finish, for example, makes the colour appear paler, and you may need to opt for a slightly darker shade. Experiment, and enjoy – who said that neutrals were boring?

CHOOSING AND USING NEUTRALS

Pure white
Clean, fresh and airy, brilliant white makes rooms appear bigger and brighter, but it can also be stark and cold.

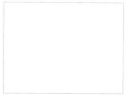

Dove
Pale greys are chic and subtle, and are beautiful with natural materials such as wicker and stone.

Stone
Mid-greys can be tough and industrial. If this look is not for you, soften with touches of lemon, pink or blue for a fashion-forward palette.

Slate
Dramatic almost-blacks make a real design statement. They are especially eye-catching when combined with splashes of bold colour.

Black
Strong and architectural, black can be used in small doses to create depth and definition in a room.

Taupe
An off-white with a definite colour but neither too yellow nor too grey, taupe makes a sophisticated background shade.

Sand
Yellowish off-whites have distinct character and add interest to a room. They will clash if used with pinkish off-whites.

Bark
Mid-browns can be warm and nurturing, reflecting the natural world – just think timber, earth and cork.

Ivory
A cool off-white, ivory looks clean and smart pretty much everywhere, and works with any other colour.

Cream
A warm off-white will cheer up a north- or east-facing room and is very easy to live with.

Magnolia
A versatile pinkish-white that was once hugely popular but is now somewhat passé. Useful for warming up a room – just don't overdo it.

Chocolate
Deep, dark and delicious, chocolate is best used in small doses (though contains no calories).

APPEALING PASTELS AND BRILLIANT BRIGHTS

Transform a room instantly by changing its colours: pale and pretty or bold and dramatic, it's time to inject instant individuality.

For some, combining colours comes naturally. For others, it helps to know a little theory first. Art books often show a colour wheel, divided into sections for the primary colours (red, blue and yellow), secondaries (purple, green and orange) and tertiaries (mixes of the above). All you need to know is that colours that are adjacent to or opposite one another on the colour wheel will co-ordinate – sometimes unexpectedly, such as fuchsia with crimson, lime green with pink, or blue with orange. And darker and lighter shades of the same colour always work well together – for example, you could put a range of blues together, from palest duck egg to rich navy.

COLOUR INSPIRATION

For some less technical colour ideas, just get outside and observe naturally occurring palettes such as a floral border, a hedgerow or the feathers of a bird. Inside, look at the furnishings you already have – are there shades you can pick out to use elsewhere? What colours feel right with the architecture of your property? Remember that muted colours tend to work best in older houses – and that paint companies often have special 'historic' ranges. What colours will show off each room to its best advantage? 'Warm' colours, for example, are good in north-facing rooms, and you can usually get away with bolder or darker colours in large, light rooms. Last of all, don't forget practical considerations: painting the lower half of your hall in a dark colour, for example, might be a good idea if you have children or pets, while a very bright colour could be too distracting in a home office. Take your time and make your colour choices count. Your home will be the happier for it.

The bold colour accents in this clean, modern scheme have been inspired by the striped fabric that has been incorporated into the soft furnishings throughout.

CHOOSING AND USING COLOURS

Rose
Pretty and feminine, pale pink is perfect for a bedroom or little girl's room. Combine with pale grey or ivory for a smarter look.

Crimson
Not easy to live with as an all-over colour, bright red is great for drawing attention to focal points within a room.

Deep red
Darker reds are a cosy and warming choice for a dining room or formal sitting room. They look lovely with natural timber and stone.

Pale blue
Pale blues are calming and relaxing. Because they seem to recede, they make small or narrow rooms appear larger.

Celadon
This pale shade is on the verge between blue and green. Always appealing, its wateriness makes it ideal for a bathroom scheme.

Rich blue
The most popular colour in the world, blue is especially calming and relaxing – and is often used for bathrooms and bedrooms.

Navy
A strong colour, which is always smart and savvy, navy blue is a classic choice.

Egg yolk
What could be nicer than a warm, sunny yellow? Mellow and inviting, it also teams well with white for a crisper effect.

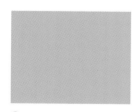

Orange
Used to add a dash of vibrant intensity, bright orange has a retro vibe and a definite feel-good factor.

Teal
Exotic and beautiful, teal can be warming and comforting. Team it with bright white for a standout accent shade.

Leaf
Wholesome, soothing and stress-busting – a good choice for a space in which you want to relax and unwind.

Lilac
Delicate and feminine, pale purples combine blue and red, which makes them cool and fresh as well as warm and welcoming.

PATTERN

It's not as hard as you may think to make patterns look great in your space.
These hints are designed to help you to take the plunge.

Are you worried about venturing away from the safety of plains? Well, set your concerns aside, because it really is easy when you know how. You can introduce pattern in all sorts of ways, from the print on a vase to a whole feature wall, a small cushion to an eye-catching rug, a lampshade to a fabulous curtain. Don't be nervous: follow a few straightforward pattern guidelines and simply take it step by step.

1 Narrow down your pattern choices by working out which styles you like best. Check out wallpaper and fabric pattern books in decorating stores, look through magazines and books, and don't be afraid to borrow ideas from other sources, such as friends' homes, restaurants, shops, galleries and hotels.

2 Would you prefer just a dash of pattern to enliven an otherwise plain room, or a striking combination of patterns for an all-over look? If you are feeling tentative, start slowly, and build it up in layers as your confidence increases.

3 In bigger rooms, large-scale patterns have amazing impact, while smaller rooms are better suited to medium- or small-scale patterns – unless you want to make a particular feature out of a tiny room by adding a dramatically huge pattern, of course.

4 Make a mood board (see pages 94–95) to ensure that your patterns work perfectly together. Try to obtain the largest possible samples of fabric and wallpaper and, before you make any final decisions, hang them in place to get a really good idea of their effect.

5 Match the key colours of your patterns exactly and the overall look will co-ordinate effortlessly.

6 Bear in mind that loose, open patterns give a visual 'breather', while intricate patterns with closely placed designs have more drama. A variety of densities give balance and interest. The same goes for scale, too.

7 Don't forget that very small patterns are only really noticeable close up; from a distance they look like a plain colour.

8 Not sure what patterns go with what? Limit your combinations to designs that originate from the same era or stylistic aesthetic.

9 Stripes are the workhorses of the pattern world. Match the colours and they will co-ordinate brilliantly with more intricate patterns.

10 Keep experimenting. Try putting a few patterns together and, if they don't look quite right, change them round until you achieve the look you want.

TYPES OF PATTERN

Pinstripe
Slim, parallel stripes, often on a dark background. Typical of men's suiting but looks smart in an interior.

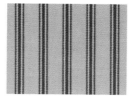

Ticking
A medium stripe on a white background often used for mattress covers. A nostalgic and simple look.

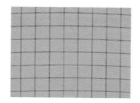

Windowpane
Slim, single-colour stripes criss-cross to form a pattern of very large checks.

Polka dot
A playful pattern of small spots, placed closely together on a plain background.

Tartan
Alternating bands of colour create a distinctive check usually associated with Scottish kilts.

Gingham
Small checks made by coloured horizontal and vertical stripes of the same width on a white background.

Hound's tooth
Small check design with a jagged shape. Traditionally twill, woven in black and white.

Herringbone
This weave is made of small zigzags. In a larger form it is similar to a chevron pattern.

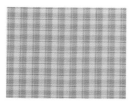

Madras
Originating in India, this informal pattern features colourful stripes that cross to form uneven checks.

Toile de Jouy
Originally from France, these patterns show pastoral scenes, often in dark red, blue or black, on a pale background.

Paisley
Of Persian or Indian origin, these patterns feature the distinctive boteh, a teardrop-shaped motif.

Ikat
Tie-dyed yarns are woven into distinctive patterns that are often based around zigzags or diamond shapes.

TEXTURE

How does your space feel? It's textures that turn a space from frumpy
to fabulous and really bring a room to life.

A varied and interesting use of texture underpins every design scheme. To an extent, we do it without thinking – putting a knitted throw over the arm of a leather sofa, or placing a wicker basket beside a stone fire surround, for example – but it is still worth taking a moment or two to ensure that your room contains a pleasing variety of interesting textures. Because not only is the right surface in the right area a functional necessity, but textures enable us to relate to our surroundings in a way that is instinctive, comforting and down-to-earth.

TALKING TEXTURE

In most rooms, the backbone textures are smooth and understated – perhaps wooden floorboards, linen upholstery and papered walls – and the interest lies in how these are combined with other elements. To make a bedroom cosier, for example, you could add a fluffy rug,

velvet curtains and quilted eiderdowns. Or, to emphasise a bright and airy living room, finishing touches might include sheer curtains, feather-trimmed cushions and glass or chrome lamp bases. If you use understated colour schemes and simple patterns, your textures will speak for themselves: sisal, shell, stone, driftwood or wicker – all beautiful, subtle and natural textures with masses of character.

Texture has an important part to play in the overall style of a room, too. Modern rooms tend to feature harder, shinier surfaces (stainless steel, chrome and mirror), whereas a vintage or ethnic look (with quilts, knitting, embroidery and lace) is more rustic and varied in texture.

A textural rug and cushions add another dimension to this understated decorative scheme.

VARIETIES OF TEXTURE

Linen
The slightly nubby, lustrous surface of woven linen gives it a lovely, subtle interest.

Leather
Natural yet hardwearing, leather has subtle creases and wrinkles that add personality.

Riven slate
Tough, long-lasting and durable, slate comes in a variety of surfaces – the riven texture has a craggy, cracked appeal.

Glazed ceramic
Ultra-smooth and ultra-shiny, glazed ceramic reflects light and contrasts well with soft fabrics.

Cashmere
Super-soft and luxurious, this expensive fibre is the ultimate in cosiness.

Coir matting
Nubby, hairy, rough and tough, coir is just one of many natural floorings that come in a variety of weaves and finishes.

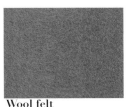

Wool felt
Thick and soft, felted wool is natural, even rustic, and offers a feeling of warmth and nostalgia.

Flokati
Flokati rugs have a deep-pile, hairy surface that feels cosy underfoot.

Velvet
Velvet is soft, warm and luxurious to the touch, thanks to its short raised pile. Combines nicely with smoother surfaces.

Silk satin
A really smooth and shiny, lustrous surface. Contrast with rougher textures – such as a satin trim on a woollen blanket.

Chrome
Super shiny, hard and reflective, chromed metal works well as a highlight in a modern scheme.

Fake fur
Fur has immediate appeal when you want a surface that is incredibly soft and comforting.

MOODBOARDS

The process of choosing all the different elements for your decorative
scheme can be mind-blowing. Help is at hand in the form of a moodboard –
a visual collage – that will help you to pin down the right look.

It's not always easy making decisions that you have to
live with for some time. However, once the planning is
over, it's time to consider flooring, wall finishes, lighting,
window treatments and furniture, and then pictures, rugs,
decorative objects and lamps. In creating a moodboard,
you will be grouping all your ideas together; it is an
excellent way of foreseeing if your designs and plans can
work. With all your ideas in one place, you can begin to
edit; it helps you to move forward.

Think about the style you want to create – you may
want to refer back to earlier pages on style and influences
(pages 22–29) and planning stages (pages 30–37).
Individual style requires confidence: go for what you like –
a moodboard allows you to experiment a little to try and
find the look you really want. Nonetheless, always bear
in mind a sense of place, what the room is to be used for,
and keep the idea of comfort and warmth in the back of
your mind. There is nothing relaxing about uncomfortable
chairs, even though they may look amazing. Spend
most on things that receive the most wear, and then add
personality and fashion to those elements that can easily
be changed – fabrics, wall colour, rugs and lampshades,
for example; it also helps to avoid expensive mistakes.

Interior designers use
moodboards to explain
design ideas to their clients.

HOW TO MAKE A MOODBOARD

Creating a moodboard will help to ensure that all the elements you have
chosen for a room makeover will look good together.

INSPIRATION AND INFLUENCES

Inspiration plays a large part in any creative process, but
sometimes you can lose track of what has inspired or
influenced you – one of the reasons why moodboards
are so successful in any interior project – we all need
direction. Try to keep your influences as wide-ranging
as possible, use interior design magazines, brochures
and photographs, tear out images that inspire you or
print them from the Internet, but also think about your
favourite restaurant, a film set or an advertisement. Go
window shopping, making notes of likes and dislikes. Take
home the largest carpet samples and fabric swatches you
can, and live with them in the room you are decorating.
Avoid buying anything on a whim. Don't be worried about
taking a rug to a showroom to match a paint colour –
it's important that things go together. Sit in your room
with your samples laid out and see if they are working.
Take your time, you need to know more about the main
elements before committing to them.

PRACTICALITIES

Before compiling your moodboard, keep all your objects,
samples and swatches together in a 'mood box'. It can be a
good idea to have two boxes: a concept box (to help define
your inspiration and style) and a sample box (materials and
finishes). Then you can start bringing the two together; a
plan of action will gradually unfold and you will soon find
out whether things relate to how you actually live.

Either use a large piece of card or a noticeboard – cork
or felt, or even an aluminium magnetic board – to pin
down your samples. For those who love the tactile nature
of fabrics and the true colour of actual paint samples, a
physical board is ideal.

Alternatively, if you are happiest in front of a computer
screen then why not use a website, such as Pinterest,
which allows you to 'pin' your ideas onto your own digital
page – it's simple to gather images from retailers' websites
or blogs and put them on your own board. The site is

absolutely vast and ever-growing, providing a library
of ideas, advice and visual references. Along with such
websites, there is a range of apps available to use when
you're out and about.

Whatever method you use, by pinning down your
ideas you will learn how to successfully create a design-
inspired interior.

STORAGE

Good storage can really improve your quality of life: tidying up is quicker and easier, and your home is more spacious and attractive.

TEN GOLDEN RULES OF STORAGE

1 You can never have too much storage. Aim for it to take up about 10–20% of each room.

2 Plan storage with military precision – it's really worth taking an hour or so to add up what's going to go where and how much space it will require.

3 Don't store items you no longer need. Regularly assess what's vital to your life and, if something's not, sell it, throw it or give it away (See Clear that clutter, below right).

4 If you only need things on rare occasions, store them in attics, basements, sheds or the tops of cupboards. Keep easy-access storage space for the stuff you need all the time.

5 Store small things in small containers and large things in larger containers.

6 Don't place heavy items higher than shoulder height or lower than knee height.

7 Storing things on open shelves is great if you are really tidy and enjoy dusting. If not, fit cupboard doors or use attractive boxes or baskets.

8 Do things keep ending up in the wrong place? Then rethink your storage. A kitchen cupboard might be a better place for toddler toys than a bedroom, for example.

9 Stacking boxes look great and save space – but if you need to get at the contents quickly and easily, don't put them in the bottom boxes.

10 Everyone has an odds and ends drawer (or several), but try not to let yours overflow out of control.

Clear that clutter

▶ Aim to declutter one room per week – or perhaps spend ten minutes decluttering each day. That way it won't be too painful.

▶ Find at least six large bags or boxes, and mark them as follows: 'rubbish', 'recycle', 'give away', 'sell', 'mend' and 'store'. You may also think of other categories that apply to you.

▶ With the bags or boxes near at hand, the sorting becomes simple. And when all you have left is the 'store' container, think carefully about the best place to keep each object. With all that unnecessary clutter out of the way, you will be amazed at how much extra space you can create.

HALLWAYS AND LIVING ROOMS

When thinking about your storage needs, tackle each room individually.
Start by making a smart entrance to your home with a well-planned hallway,
and creating order in your living room.

A NEAT AND TIDY HALL

When space is tight, a useful hallway option is a set of shallow, floor-to-ceiling cupboards with plain doors, (painted the same colour as the walls, or mirrored to maximise light) ranked along one wall. For books or an out-of-the-way display, a shelf running the length of the hallway, above head height, works really well. Add a place for post and keys – perhaps a small, wall-mounted cupboard, or a bowl on a shelf and a set of hooks. Don't forget the space beneath the staircase – if you are not already using it as a home office or extra loo, it can be your most essential, multi-purpose cupboard, efficiently equipped with shelves, baskets and hooks.

ORGANISED LIVING

For CDs and DVDs, books and magazines, shelving is vital to keep your living room neat and tidy, and the obvious place to fit it is across the alcoves either side of a chimney breast. Fit cupboard doors (solid or glazed) in front of the lower shelves for extra versatility. Alternatively, freestanding bookshelves, as tall as possible for maximum storage, can be placed anywhere there is floor and wall space. A chest that doubles up as a coffee table is a handy option and, if you are buying a side table, choose one with slim drawers to accommodate remote controls,

Fitted or freestanding storage?

Built-in, fitted storage is neater and takes up less room than freestanding pieces. It can cover walls or span alcoves, but is also ideal for awkward spaces such as above doors, under sloping ceilings and beneath bay windows. Think open shelves, cupboards, drawers or whatever suits your needs – designed so as to echo architectural details (such as architraves or door panels) elsewhere in the room. Keep costs down by using pine, chipboard or medium-density fibreboard, and finish with primer, undercoat and eggshell paint.

However, freestanding storage can be moved around and is often less expensive than commissioning fitted pieces. Choose a style to suit your interior – anything from an antique Oriental chest to a modern designer sideboard. Found a cheap piece with an ugly veneer? A coat of paint will redeem it. Second-hand finds can be transformed by stripping, painting and changing pulls, knobs or handles. And don't forget smaller storage – boxes and baskets, hooks and hanging rails – to tidy up awkwardly shaped stuff that won't go anywhere else.

Fitted cupboards in hallways provide neat storage for shoes and coats.

A mix of open shelves and cupboards with doors works well in a living room.

When your storage is glass-fronted, make sure what's inside is kept neat and tidy.

BATHROOMS AND KITCHENS

For the most practical, functional rooms in the house, such as kitchens and bathrooms, excellent storage is vital. A combination of tried-and-tested solutions and ingenious ideas will help you keep clutter under control.

AN ORDERLY KITCHEN

Get clever in the kitchen and you will find endless options for well-designed storage. In general, try to use the walls as much as possible, going high with full-height cupboards and larders, and utilising unused spaces between wall units and worktops with hanging racks, rails and shelves. Instead of hinged cupboards, base-level drawers in a range of depths allow easier access to contents, while internal divisions help you get better organised. 'Magic corner' cupboards are enormously helpful, and don't forget that shallow storage units can be hung on the back of a broom cupboard or understairs door to hold anything from a mop to vacuum cleaner accessories.

BLISSFUL BATHROOMS

To get the best from your bathroom you need it to be both an oasis for blissful bathing and a functional and efficient space. But it will be neither if you don't get your storage right. The solution is to display only your most attractive accessories, and conceal all the boring or unattractive stuff well out of the way. Make a start with a wall-mounted cupboard or a vanity unit below the basin and add open shelves for folded towels, pretty bottles and the like. Over-the-door hooks and hanging pockets provide masses of storage but take up very little room, as do corner-fitting units, shower shelves with suction pads and storage towers on wheels.

Storage included below sinks helps to conceal messy bathroom clutter and keep surfaces clear.

HOW TO PUT UP A SHELF
IN AN ALCOVE

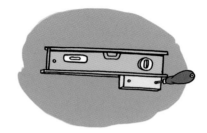

Before you start
Check the walls for wires and pipes using a cable detector. Wear safety goggles and a dust mask when drilling or sawing. For plasterboard walls, you will have to screw your battens to the studs behind the plasterboard.

Using a spirit level, draw a pencil line around the inside of the alcove to mark the lower edge of the shelf. Cut lengths of 50 x 25mm (2 x 1in) timber to fit, angling the front ends of the side battens at 45° so they will be less obvious once fitted.

Drill pilot holes every 250mm (10in) on the timber batten. Hold the batten against the back wall just below the pencil line and mark where the fixing holes will be. Drill and plug the holes, then attach the batten to the wall using screws that are at least 50mm (2in) long. Repeat for the two side battens.

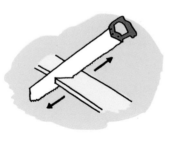

Repeat steps 1 and 2 for the remaining shelves in the alcove, then cut the shelves to the correct size – measuring both the front and back of each shelf space accurately for a good fit.

If the shelf does not quite fit against the back wall, you may need to scribe it: use a block of wood taped to a pencil to trace the outline of the wall on the shelf, then saw, plane or sand along the line.

For extra stability, nail, screw or glue the shelves into position. Prime and paint.

BEDROOMS

A bedroom should be a relaxing retreat, which means that well thought-out storage is especially important. The same goes for children's rooms, where smart thinking will help you keep up with their ever-changing requirements.

A CALMING BEDROOM

How much bedroom storage do you need? Most people underestimate the amount required, and the only real answer is to take a tape measure and plan it out. Wardrobes fitted wall-to-wall and floor-to-ceiling make the best use of space. Decide whether you need full, half or three-quarter hanging space, and then you will be able to add shelves, drawers, racks or stacking boxes according to how much space you have left. Other options include hanging a shoe rack behind the door, using a small cabinet as a bedside table and employing the large space under the bed for trunks, suitcases or underbed boxes on wheels.

KEEPING KIDS' KIT IN CHECK

A combination of open shelves and cupboards is the answer to the incredible mess that can quickly be generated in most children's room. Keep things at child-height, avoid 'themes' that will quickly be outgrown, and screw shelves and wardrobes securely to the wall. In a small room, a raised bed provides great space for both storage and study. To maximise floor area, employ peg rails, hooks, stacking boxes and hanging fabric organisers. Avoid heavy-lidded toy boxes that can trap fingers – coloured plastic buckets are much better. And one last tip: labelling or colour co-ordinating boxes or shelves will make tidying much easier.

TYPES OF STORAGE

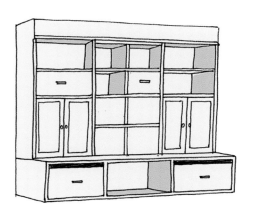

Modular storage

Comprises units of different types – drawers, shelves and cupboards – that fit together to create a personalised storage system.

Built-in storage

An expensive option but worth it if you have awkward spaces to fill. It is also completely bespoke so you can choose whatever storage option you like.

Freestanding storage

Can be moved to different sites within a room or between different rooms if you decide you want a change. Usually combines cupboards and drawers.

Organisers

Fit within existing storage to keep items in order, such as shoes, clothes, toys and paperwork. Can include boxes, hanging storage or inserts for drawers.

PLANNING MAKES PERFECT

If you want a home that functions perfectly and looks gorgeous,
careful planning is the key.

Good planning means considering every aspect of your interior design, from who will do the work, to what materials, furnishings and finishing touches you need to buy. It means drawing up a budget, understanding rules and regulations and getting to grips with safety. It may mean employing a professional, or learning a new skill. And it means the most exciting thing of all – that you are getting started!

FIRST THINGS FIRST

Although you may be tempted to rush in and try to change everything at once, now is the time to stand back and take some sensible decisions. Is the property structurally safe and sound? Is it warm enough in winter? Have you got plenty of hot water whenever you need it? Do your windows stick when you try to open them? Are your stairs creaky or is your plaster crumbling away? Before you do anything decorative, it is much more important to focus on repairs and renovations. Buy a new boiler before the three-piece suite (better to be cosy on an old sofa than freezing on a new one) and mend your gutters before you repaint. In the long run, you will be happy that you got your priorities right.

Make good the structure of your property
before starting any decorating project.

REPAIRS AND RENOVATIONS

Before you embark on a decorating project, make sure your home is as sound
as it can be. Here are a few common problems to watch out for.

CRACKS IN WALLS

Cracks are often caused by tiny movements of your
house and may be nothing to worry about. However, you
should get professional advice from a qualified chartered
surveyor if a crack is more than 5mm (¼in) wide, if it keeps
getting bigger, if you have more than one crack in a room,
or if a crack appears outside as well as inside.

CREAKING STAIRS

Creaks are caused by timbers moving and rubbing
against each other. First, identify which tread is causing
the problem. If you can get at the staircase from below,
it should be quite easy to glue and screw the wedges
that hold the tread in place. If not, then try screwing up
through the riser at an angle so as to secure it to the tread
above. Or use steel corner braces. Squirting wood glue
into gaps may also help.

STICKING OR RATTLING SASH WINDOWS

Old sash windows need regular attention: if you are
confident in your skills, you could dismantle, ease, adjust,
re-cord and reassemble them; if not, there are a number
of specialist companies who can do it for you. Draught-
proof them at the same time (see right).

DAMP PATCHES

These are often caused by blocked, cracked or
disconnected gutters, downpipes or drains. Sort these out
first. Check for leaking plumbing, and cracks in external
walls, too. Rising damp is often caused by the ground
level outside being too high. Reduce it in order to let
the wall breathe. If you have mould on cold surfaces,
especially in bathrooms or cupboards, the damp is caused
by condensation. Improve heating and ventilation, and it
should be resolved.

DRAUGHTS

Try draught-proofing strips around windows and doors
– the best option is a specialist seal fitted into a cut-in
rebate (compression seals for hinged windows; wipers for
sliding sashes). Shutters or heavy, floor-to-ceiling curtains
are also effective. For windows that you seldom open,
secondary glazing is ideal. Cover keyholes, letter slots and
cat flaps on external doors, and add an old-fashioned
'sausage dog' along the bottom edge. Seal gaps at the
base of the skirting boards with foam strips, silicon mastic
or thin slivers of matching timber. To fill gaps between old
floorboards, use fillets of balsa wood or lengths of string,
which can be stained, glued and pushed into place.

LEAKING ROOF

Stand away from the house and use binoculars to check
the roof tiles, chimney stack, rainwater goods, mortar and
flashing (lead or zinc sheet that covers joins between roof
and walls or chimney). Then go into the loft and check
that timbers are dry and solid and there are no damp
patches on the ceiling. You may be able to safely clear
gutters and repair downpipes, but most rooftop jobs
should be left to a professional.

BLOCKED CHIMNEYS

Poorly maintained fireplaces and flues are the biggest
causes of fires in old buildings. Have your chimney
swept regularly, and use a smoke pellet to check it for air
tightness. If your flue is faulty and cannot be mended from
outside, or if you are fitting a stove, you will need to install
a flue liner first.

DOING IT YOURSELF

Doing it yourself is fun and economical, until something goes wrong, that is.
If you have the skills, the time and the right tools or equipment, DIY is great.
If not, you'll need to bite the bullet and GSI (get someone in).

HOW TO LEARN DIY

- **DIY parent:** A patient parent who knows what he or she is doing – and will even lend you the right tool if you haven't got it – is ideal. If you haven't got a DIY parent, perhaps you have a handy friend or neighbour who would be prepared to show you the basics.
- **Classes:** Adult education classes are a great place in which to learn all sorts of DIY skills, from introductory courses to professional qualifications, from an experienced teacher with all necessary tools at hand.
- **The Internet:** DIY videos posted on the internet can be really helpful. Just make sure you choose one that comes from a reliable source.
- **Books, magazines and leaflets:** They are no substitute for the personal touch, but you can still glean plenty of basic information, as well as tips and tricks, from written sources. Specific in-store advice leaflets can often be particularly good.

DIY or GSI?

- How handy are you (be honest)? If you don't have the aptitude, don't be tempted to try anything too tricky.
- Is your toolbox up to the job? Basic kit is fine for many projects, but more complex tasks may require other tools, which you will need to buy or hire.
- Do you live in an older property? Uneven walls and floors make even straightforward DIY more challenging.
- Have you got the time? It is easy to underestimate how long it will take to complete a job, especially if you have never done it before.
- Does the project involve heavy lifting? Don't be a hero – get someone to help.
- Does it involve gas or electricity? Then don't hesitate to call in a professional.

TOOLBOX BASICS

Tape measure
A 5m length is useful. Buy one that is easy to read, lockable and that retracts easily.

Claw hammer
Both for driving in nails and levering them out. Available in different sizes and weights – 16oz is a good general choice.

Pliers
Look for comfortable grips that are insulated against electric shocks. Standard pliers for general use; fine nose for fiddly jobs.

Set of screwdrivers
Cross-headed and flat-headed, in a range of sizes, for different uses around the home.

Set of Allen keys
It's amazing how many items need one of these little keys to tighten or loosen them.

Hacksaw
For small jobs, a junior hacksaw is fine, and will cut plastic, metal and small pieces of wood. Buy a set of spare blades, too.

Trimming knife
These have replaceable, retractable blades. A standard blade will cut thinner materials; special blades cut wood, laminates and metal.

Spirit level
This is essential to make sure your work is straight. A 600mm level is a good length.

Adjustable spanner
Use it with a variety of nuts and bolts; 10in is a good size.

Paint brushes
At least five sizes is useful (1, 1½, 2, 2½ and 3in). Choose natural bristles for oil-based paints, or synthetic for use with water-based paints.

Paint roller and tray
Short-pile rollers are ideal for flat surfaces; medium for slightly uneven surfaces; long for exterior or textured surfaces.

Torch
Essential when working in dark corners, or when your power has gone off.

SAFETY

Never take shortcuts where safety is concerned. Some DIY jobs can be
hazardous, especially if you haven't had a great deal of experience or training.
Use your common sense and avoid accidents.

- ▶ Always use the right tool for the job. Don't be tempted to bodge – not only could it be risky, but the work is unlikely to turn out well.
- ▶ If you have hired a tool you're not familiar with, read the operating instructions carefully and, if in doubt, ask for a run-through before you leave the hire shop.
- ▶ Use cordless power tools when possible. When using one with a cord, check that the cord is in good condition, and use a circuit breaker.
- ▶ Lift heavy weights with care: keep your back straight and bend from the knee. Get help if necessary.
- ▶ Ladders are a major cause of accidents. Place on firm, even ground and ask someone to hold the bottom. The golden rule is to keep three limbs in contact with the ladder at all times. Never over-reach. Get help when using an extension ladder.
- ▶ Never use tools that are blunt or broken.
- ▶ Wear appropriate clothing – sensible shoes with good grips, shirts that don't flap about, goggles, a dust mask and ear defenders when necessary. Tie long hair out of the way and take off jewellery.
- ▶ When painting, using toxic materials or creating lots of dust, keep the room well ventilated.

Rules and regulations

Small changes to the design of your interior are unlikely to concern your local planning department, but if you are considering bigger alterations, such as an extension or loft conversion, you may need to get planning permission. And if your building is listed or if you live in a conservation area, be extra careful to check what you can and can't do.

Building regulations cover practically every aspect of building work to your home, from the energy efficiency of new windows to electrical installations, and it is important that you comply with them. You can usually leave this aspect of the work to the professional you employ, but if you are doing it yourself, check with the building control department of your local authority.

- Don't smoke while doing DIY, and keep children and pets away from your working area.
- Plan your work in advance. Don't rush or cut corners.
- Clear up as soon as possible once you have finished, and store tools and equipment safely.
- Keep a first-aid kit and a fire extinguisher handy, just in case.

HOME IMPROVEMENT JOBS TO TACKLE YOURSELF

- Painting.
- Tiling and grouting.
- Making curtains, blinds and cushion covers.
- Wallpapering.
- Putting up a shelf.
- Sanding floorboards.
- Filling holes and cracks in walls.
- Repairing patches of rotten woodwork.
- Laying laminate flooring.
- Bleeding radiators.
- Insulating the loft.

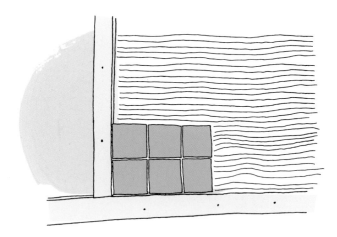

Sanding floors and tiling walls are two home improvement jobs you can do yourself.

GETTING THE BUILDERS IN

Whether you are converting a loft or fitting a new cupboard, a skilled and reliable tradesperson is worth his or her weight in gold.

When you hire a builder you must establish a professional and good-natured working relationship, in which everyone knows who is responsible for what, and exactly how each task will be carried out. Good builders are able to advise and help solve problems – but remember, it is your money and your home, so the final decisions must be yours. Ensure that your plans are fully developed, down to the last detail, before work starts.

THE SPECIALISTS: WHO DOES WHAT?

▸ **Architects** design buildings, extensions and renovations, and produce specifications and technical drawings for the contractors. They advise on whether the plans for your property will require planning permission and/or need to comply with building regulations.

▸ **Quantity surveyors** manage the costs on larger projects.

▸ **Structural engineers** work with architects to ensure that new structures or alterations are safe.

▸ **Project managers** are responsible for the planning, design, execution, monitoring and closure of a project.

▸ **Main contractors** provide the material, labour and equipment to carry out a project.

▸ **Sub-contractors** include plumbers, electricians, tilers or glaziers, and are often employed by main contractors for specialist tasks.

▸ **Interior designers** plan spaces for function, comfort and good looks.

Workmen on site

When you are employing a tradesperson, it is important to get the details sorted out in advance. Try to establish the following to avoid clashes with neighbours or yourself before the job gets started:

▸ The order of work.

▸ What hours they will arrive and leave.

▸ How they will get in and who locks up (if you're not living there).

▸ Where they can park and store equipment.

▸ Who will clear out the working areas in advance.

▸ Who will clear the mess up afterwards.

▸ What loo they can use.

▸ Where they can clean their tools.

▸ Whether or not they can play a radio.

▸ Whether they can bring pets to the property.

Finding a good builder

It's the eternally worrying question: how to find a good builder (or plumber, or electrician, or tiler – or even an architect, or interior designer). Before you take anyone on, check that they are properly qualified and have adequate insurance for the job. You could also ask for references from previous clients.

▸ **Personal recommendation:** If friends, family or neighbours have had work done recently and were happy with it, grab the details without hesitation.

▸ **Professional and trade associations:** Look up the relevant association and you can often simply type in your postcode to be given a list of local members. Some associations offer guarantee schemes.

▸ **The Internet:** A variety of sites offer to find you a good local builder, often by recommendation. Check out their credentials first, though.

▸ **Local paper:** Small ads can be a great source of local tradespeople but, as with the internet, you'll need to check them out before hiring them.

▸ **Local building works:** See a skip outside a nearby house? Pluck up your courage and politely ask the house owner whether they would recommend their builder. They will probably be only too happy to share their experiences with you.

THE WORK PLAN

For a smooth-running project and successful end results, make sure that every aspect of any home improvement work is carefully planned.

Co-ordinating the work so that everything happens in the right order will avoid hold-ups, duplication of work, extra expense, and above all it will give you peace of mind. Here is a general guide to the sequence of works, whether you're building an extension or carrying out internal works. If you are project managing the work, determine which point on this list is relevant to your particular needs and follow from that point onwards (missing out any that don't apply). Even if you're only working on one room, it's helpful to keep to the list because it won't change regardless of the size of the project. If your builder acts as the contractor then this will be his or her responsibility.

SEQUENCE OF WORK

- **Planning permission:** Obtain any necessary permissions and consents.
- **Clear the decks:** Move furniture, curtains, rugs, carpets etc. out of the way. Get rid of any that you won't be using and store the rest.
- **Knocking down:** Remove any structures or old service as required. Arrange for a skip to remove rubble, if necessary.
- **Preventative or curative treatments:** Check damp-proof course, add a new one, if necessary. Remove rotten timber, spray against rot or pest infestation. Sweep chimneys and flues, if required.
- **External services:** Install major external connections to services – water, gas, electricity and telephone cables.
- **Basic construction:** Dig foundations and lay drains. Build new walls and lay solid floors. Then build upper floor or roof structure, as necessary, and cover as quickly as possible.
- **Services:** Install services (those that are mostly hidden), such as boilers, pipework, electrical conduits, and drains from sanitary fittings.
- **First finishes:** Carpentry work should be done next, door frames and windows, studwork and floor joists. Plaster the walls. Tile floors, glaze windows, add doors and skirting.

- **Fitting out:** Install bathrooms, baths, showers and basins. Fit socket plates, radiators, fuse boxes. Some of this work may not take place until after decoration is finished. Add built-in fixtures and fittings, such as bedroom wardrobes, fitted cupboards and fixed shelving. Fit new kitchen units and appliances.
- **Decoration:** Paint (or wallpaper) walls, ceilings and woodwork. Fit curtain tracks or poles. Add the last fittings – door handles, window catches and locks.
- **Furnishings:** Lay carpets; hang pendant lights; fit curtains and blinds; put furniture in position; hang pictures and mirrors.

CHANGING ROOMS

Making the best use of the space at your disposal by changing the function
of a room can make all the difference to how you live.

When it comes to our homes, we are often slaves to traditional layouts, with bedrooms upstairs, living rooms downstairs, kitchens at the rear of the house, and so on. But there's no reason why you can't have a living room upstairs, especially if there is a wonderful view out of the window. Use your imagination and think about how the existing space in your home could be improved, in terms of working or looking better. Assess whether rooms are achieving their full potential: is there a room that is under-used, for example, or one that is unsafe for children, or not ideally situated for an elderly family member.

FIRST THOUGHTS

If you are thinking about changing the function of a room, think through the practical issues at the start – certain rooms will require more work than others. As well as services (electricity, gas, heating), fittings, such as windows, doors, fireplaces and lighting, should be considered first. Ask yourself questions about the room, such as: does the room have enough natural light for its new purpose? And does the existing lighting serve the needs of the new?

Of course, if you're thinking about moving a kitchen or bathroom, plumbing and drainage is a high priority. Then you need to take account of the decorative elements of a room – flooring, wall coverings, window treatments. Draw up a checklist of what will need to change. For anything but a simple change of function, you are best to seek professional advice – from an architect, surveyor or builder – who will comply with all building regulations.

ROOM FOR CHANGE

Providing it does not involve moving services around, changing the function of a room is one of the simplest you can make in your home. For instance, many people no longer use formal dining rooms; kitchen-diners have become the heart of the home and are far more popular. Why not transform a dining room into an office/library (where children can do their homework), or even a spare bedroom? Either of these options are an easy home

design solution and more about decoration than having to worry about structural issues.

Similarly, why shouldn't the largest room upstairs be given to the children, rather than the parents, when the children could use it as a playroom and a bedroom?

Although it does involve moving services, a popular way of using a large bedroom to its best advantage is to divide the space into two – a smaller bedroom and a bathroom. Whichever room you decide to transform, it is worth bearing in mind adjoining rooms and spaces: they may have different characteristics that are worth respecting.

STAYING ON BUDGET

Whether your project is large or small, it is vital to keep
in careful control of your costs.

Start by deciding who is going to do the work. If it is
possible to do it yourself, you will save money – provided
you can do it properly. If you need to employ a builder or
other tradesperson for anything other than the smallest
of jobs, draw up a specification in advance, covering both
the labour and the materials required, meet the people
on site, and get at least three quotes (not estimates).
Remember that the cheapest quote is not always the best.

THE DOS AND DON'TS OF BUDGETING

▶ **DO** try to think of everything. It's worth making the
effort at the beginning to plan every last detail. In the
long run, it will save you time, money and stress.

▶ **DON'T** change your mind or add extra work halfway
through your project. It will irritate your builder and
end up costing you more.

▶ **DO** be realistic with your budget. If you are overly
optimistic about costs, you are bound to get
caught out.

▶ **DO** allow at least a 10% contingency. Unfortunately,
unexpected problems are a fact of life.

▶ **DO** plan to get jobs such as brickwork, tiling and
plastering all done at the same time. It should save
time, money and mess.

▶ **DON'T** forget to add in the costs of obtaining planning
permission and alternative accommodation, if you have
to move out while the work is going on.

▶ **DON'T** pay your builder upfront. Reputable builders
have accounts with trade suppliers so there should
be no need. Agree a method of payment (usually in
instalments) in writing, and stick to it.

▶ **DO** keep back 10% at the end of the work to cover
possible defects. When everything is complete, make
a list of 'snags' and ask your builder to remedy them.
Pay the final amount promptly once you are satisfied.

*Buying furniture at charity
shops or on online auction sites
can help reduce costs.*

Three ways to reduce your costs

1 Do at least some of the work yourself
(or get a DIY-savvy friend to help).

2 Economise on materials (can you buy second-
hand, wait for a sale or get to an
outlet store?).

3 Carry out the work in stages.

TROUBLESHOOTING

Always be on the lookout for problems, such as wood rot, woodworm and
pest infestation, in a house or flat rather than waiting for them to appear.

The most common cause of damage to timber is damp
conditions and woodworm infeston; this applies to
woodwork throughout the home. At the first sign of any
rotten wood or infestation, take action to remedy the
problem before any further damage is done.

It will depend on the seriousness of the problem as
to whether you treat the rot or woodworm yourself or
seek professional help. Surveys and estimates for such
treatments are free, but can be alarming, as they leave
nothing to chance. However, they usually offer a 20-year
guarantee, so they need to be thorough. Always get more
than one survey/estimate; they can vary considerably.

CHECKING FOR WOODWORM

While there are many different types of wood-boring
insects, only experts can identify the precise species of
beetle that attacks timber. The common furniture beetle
is responsible for the majority of woodworm damage in
Britain. If you discover a series of tiny, round holes in any
woodwork you probably have or have had woodworm.

Females lay their eggs in cracks in bare wood, and
the larvae that hatch remain in the wood (burrowing
destructively for up to three years), eventually leaving via a
small flight hole. To test whether the grubs are still around,
simply tap the timber with a hammer or mallet, and if
fine white powder or dust comes out of the holes, the
little devils are probably still in there. But if this does not
happen, don't assume that they have gone away.

If the outbreak is minor, treat the wood with an
insecticidal fluid that penetrates the wood, eradicates
the woodworm and provides long-term protection
against further attacks. The preservative normally
contains a fungicide that gives protection against
fungal attack, too. Brush a generous coating onto the
wooden surface and also inject the fluid into flight holes.
Follow the manufacturer's instructions very carefully as
these chemicals are hazardous. Wood that has been
heavily infested, and thus severely damaged, may need
to be replaced.

WOOD ROT

Wet and dry rot are the two main types of fungus that
attack wood. Both need moisture to develop – dry wood
is not affected by rot – the level of moisture will determine
which fungus will grow. Take expert advice on the cause of
the damp – it will usually be rising or penetrating damp,
but could be leaking plumbing – and have it remedied.

Wet rot is less alarming than dry rot. It attacks timber
with a high moisture content, such as wood that has been
saturated with water over a long period of time. However,
the fungus does not spread far from the damp area and
therefore the damage is usually far less widespread.

Know your enemy

▸ **Woodworm:** There are different types of wood-boring insects, but the natural habitat for the common furniture beetle is trees, so wood in buildings – floorboards, doors, windows and furniture – are all natural substitutes. Generally, they are most noticeable between May and October; however, they can go unseen for many years, especially in areas such as roof spaces.

▸ **Rodents:** Mice and rats gnaw on wood, plastic, cables and other hard materials, which can be a fire hazard. Look for small, dark droppings with an ammonia-like smell, especially in enclosed areas (cupboards or under sinks) and along walls.

▸ **Moths:** Preventing clothes moths from entering a home is pretty impossible. Moths lay eggs in dark, undisturbed areas – lofts, spare rooms, little-used wardrobes – where clothing or other textiles are stored; their larvae hatch and feed on fabrics. Make sure you clean textiles before storing, moths like dirty clothing. It's a good idea to put them in sealed plastic bags.

To treat, first eradicate the cause of the damp, and the fungi will die. The timbers should still be treated with a fungicidal fluid (follow manufacturer's instructions) in case the dry rot spores leap in and get a hold as the wood is drying out.

Dry rot only occurs in dark, unventilated conditions, unlike wet rot, and it attacks wood with a low moisture content. It is considered to be more serious than wet rot because the spores of dry rot fungus will spread throughout a building, even through brickwork and masonry, to infect other wood. All trace of the fungus has to be eradicated and surfaces treated over a wide area. Dry rot appears as light grey strands with a white growth like cotton wool on the wood. If you discover dry rot, call in a timber-treatment specialist.

OTHER PESTS

Other common pests, in particular rodents and moths, can damage your home and your wallet. Pest infestation can blight the lives of families, affect the sale of your property and prove costly. Every year local authority pest controllers carry out thousands of treatments for various infestations.

It's often cold weather that forces rats and mice to nest and forage for food indoors. The main problem is that they spread disease and cause damage by chewing through wiring, timber, pipes and brickwork. Rodents can be eliminated by using traps or poison, or if you prefer, you can contact your local authority or a specialist firm.

Prospective buyers can be put off by evidence of wood rot, woodworm damage and other pests. Always try to be open and accommodating. But be aware that mortgage companies can hold back funds until these problems have been remedied.

INSURANCE

When it comes to home insurance, in general most companies don't cover for damage caused by pests – that is, unless you take out a more expensive policy offering pest cover.

So when you see holes in your timber, or a mouse scampering along the skirting board, take action. In the case of woodworm, determine the source and remedy the problem. And if you have mice living in your house, make sure you get rid of them quickly.

GOING ROOM BY ROOM

HALLS, STAIRS AND LANDINGS

*Treat the hall, stairs and landing as you would other rooms in the home –
consider practicalities and functions, as well as style and visual appearance.*

Halls, stairs and landings are
fundamentally thoroughfares and
you must allow for the smooth flow
from outside to inside, from one
room to another, and from upstairs
to downstairs. When designing and
decorating, you need to be very
practical as they are areas of high
usage and subject to considerable
wear and tear. In addition, you need
to make sure there is no chance
of stumbling over furniture or
slipping on polished floors or loose
rugs, and to avoid accidents there
should be ample lighting. Keeping
their main function in mind, halls
and landings should be planned
to work well with the rest of the
house. Be clear about your personal
requirements and priorities.

VISUAL EFFECTS

Entrance halls provide the first
view of the rest of your home;
they should be warm, friendly and
welcoming. If you have a roomy
hall this makes life easier, but if you
have a relatively small hall, there are
clever ways of creating a feeling of
space. Sightlines can help to create
a bright, welcoming area with a
sense of openness. From your front
door, check to see if you can catch
a glimpse of the back garden or
greenery from a small window;
or an interesting-looking room

*Sealed wooden flooring is a
practical choice for hallways.
This scheme also incorporates
fitted cupboards for storage.*

*In this hallway design the
dramatic floor provided the
inspiration for a bold paint
effect on the walls.*

leading off the hall; or the sky from a roof light in the stairwell. Similarly, consider sightlines when choosing colours for walls and flooring; imagine how they will look next to adjacent rooms when doors are left open. Try to create flow through the home. Use mirrors in hallways to bounce light around and to create a feeling of space.

USE OF SPACE

In a small house it might seem like a good idea to get rid of the hall and open up the living space. Think twice before doing this; it may extend your floor space in one area, but a hall provides a mediating zone – a breathing space – between indoors and out. In addition, it will deprive you of privacy; people outside will be able to see straight into your home.

The space under the stairs is often used for storage, but if you're short of space it can be a really useful spot. Use it for a downstairs loo, a utility area for a washing machine and tumble dryer, or a small study area. Larger landings can also be used for compact working areas.

In a narrow corridor, don't clog up the space by positioning a line of coat hooks along the wall – move coat racks into more spacious areas or cupboards. And even if you have room for seating, a thoroughfare is unlikely to be used as a space for relaxing. However, if you do have space it might be a terrific location for a decorative piece of furniture.

Don't waste the wall space – use for pictures, collections and displays. Landings can also be used in the same way, and perhaps also for bookshelves.

Hall basics

▶ People need somewhere to wipe their feet – a large doormat is essential.
▶ A light switch just inside the door will be useful.
▶ It will be necessary to have somewhere to hang outdoor clothing. And somewhere for muddy shoes, umbrellas, roller skates, etc.
▶ A shelf or alcove where you can leave mail, messages and keys is useful.
▶ Never allow a hall to be cluttered – there must be easy access to other rooms and the stairs.
▶ Floors need to be durable and washable; consider the period and style of your house before deciding on the material. Tiles or sealed wooden flooring are excellent choices. If you decide to have carpet, make sure that the colour will not show the dirt and that it is easy to clean.
▶ Use lighting to pick out features – tables, bookshelves and pictures.
▶ Lower parts of walls are likely to get some rough treatment from bicycles, sticky fingers and pets, so use washable paint.
▶ Inspired use of colour will help you put your individual stamp on the hall, stairs and landing. In a small area, a single colour scheme over walls and woodwork can create a stunning impact. Subtle tones and complementary colours can add interest if you have panelling, moulding or alcoves. Dark halls may benefit from bolder colours.

STAIRS

Staircases often dominate halls, and while period-style or contemporary stairs can provide a dramatic statement in a home, with clever design ideas even an average staircase can become more than just a thoroughfare.

Most importantly, think about sightlines from the bottom to the top of the stairs; try to create some interest to draw the eye upstairs. Place a collection of china on a landing windowsill; put a decorative piece of furniture in an alcove. While it is impossible to line the walls of the stairs with anything that protrudes, as in halls and corridors, you can use them for collections of prints or photographs. The top of the stairwell is probably the largest wall space in the house, and an ideal location for a really large painting or well-loved quilt or tapestry.

The stairwell is also a good place to introduce a strong colour or a wallpaper design that will give you a jolt of

pleasure as you move from place to place. As you will experience this only momentarily, it means you are less likely to tire of it. And consider painting handrails and balusters in something other than white.

FLOORING FOR STAIRS AND LANDINGS

If you have carpet in the hall, then carry it up the stairs and landing for continuity, but if you have hard flooring, such as tiles or wood, you will need to consider what to have on the stairs and landings. Fitted carpet is a popular solution – it is warm and far less noisy than harder options. However, make sure that it is hardwearing and easy to clean. Alternatively – if you want to make a feature of a dull, straight stairway – choose a carpet runner, using either carpet rods or various forms of gripper, with painted or polished wooden treads at either side. Carpets, fitted or runners, come in a multitude of colours, patterns and fibres – all of which are important considerations.

For open-tread wooden stairs, make sure that they are sealed well, but with a product that does not produce a high polish or slippery surface. Painted stairs can look stunning, especially if they are the same colour as used in the hall, but be aware that they can be slippery.

STAIR SAFETY

Stairs can be hazardous. If you replace a staircase, be sure to comply with building regulations. The rules relate to size and layout of stairs and apply to all new work (but not repairs to existing stairs).

A key safety issue is lighting. Make sure staircases are well lit; low-level lighting is acceptable as long as there is a clear distinction between riser and tread. Another issue is flooring: avoid polished wooden treads – they may prove to be too slippery. Badly laid carpets can cause accidents, so make sure a professional fits them.

Finally, steps should have a maximum rise of 22cm (8½in) and rails should be a minimum of 0.9m (3ft) high for both stairs and landings.

TYPES OF STAIRCASES

Period-style staircase

Staircases with interesting architectural details should be carefully restored and simply decorated. Handrails and balusters can be treated in different ways: left as natural wood (polished or sealed); painted in one colour; or with the handrail and newel post left natural and the balusters painted a colour.

Traditional staircase with boxed-in sides

An average, traditional staircase can provide a dramatic statement; one of the best ways to encourage this is to make it as open as possible. Remove the boxed-in sides and leave open, or replace with balusters and a handrail, in wood or metal, or even glass.

Spiral staircase

Spiral stairs come in a variety of designs and materials, from ornate, period cast-iron to simpler, contemporary wood and metal versions. A spiral staircase may seem more compact than conventional stairs, but you still need an area of about 2m (6ft) square to allow for wide enough treads and, of course, you lose understair space. Spiral staircases have undeniable appeal and when they are used outside, for instance, from a first-floor flat down to a garden, they combine functionality with aesthetics.

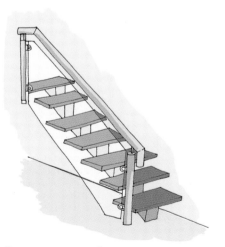

Contemporary staircase

If you are having a new staircase fitted, make sure it's visually interesting. Contemporary staircases can completely transform the look of a house. However, it will be expensive, so think twice about having a look that is too trendy – it won't necessarily last.

Positioning the handrail away from the main living area means that the space is not broken up; painting it in a light colour also maximises the feeling of openness.

It is important that the style of staircase you choose fits in with the rest of your house. These boxed-in stairs blend in well with the retro style of the room.

Completely open stairs can be unsafe. Here, vertical handrails provide stability while keeping the space open.

In a wide hallway, built-in storage is an elegant way to provide much-needed storage for the whole family.

In this hallway, a demi lune table creates a focal point. Decorative items and artwork provide interest in a space that is usually just a thoroughfare.

Don't be afraid to use colour when decorating your stairs – in open-plan spaces it can provide a focal point and link the different areas together.

LIVING ROOMS

Understanding what you want out of your living space is crucial to its success: you need to make sure the room fulfils all of its functions as well as being somewhere you want to spend your time. Careful planning is key.

PLANNING

The best way to start is with a floor plan: it will help you visualise how the various elements of the room will work together before you begin to move things around. Start with your windows and doors and also include features like plugs and radiators – these are all features that can't be moved.

POSITIONING YOUR FURNITURE

Seating area: This usually comprises the main element of a living room, and is often arranged around a focal point such as the television or a fireplace. Make sure you choose the best position for the sofa relative to the television, speakers and tables. For entertaining, it helps to have chairs grouped together, and make sure there are surfaces within easy reach for people to put drinks, etc.

Dining area: For dual-function living/dining rooms, the amount of space you dedicate to each function will depend on the size of table you need, although extendable tables are a useful way to save space when not in use. Something else to consider is the position of the dining table relative to the kitchen – the nearer the better when carrying plates. The dining area can also double up as a craft area when necessary.

Here, a children's area is defined using a colourful rug, a section of wall painted using blackboard paint, and an upcycled cupboard for storage.

A reading corner can be created using a comfortable chair and good lighting; a table within reach is also useful.

Work/study area: To enable people to work or study effectively, it helps to place the desk so that it faces away from the seating area. Making use of alcoves can provide an element of privacy and utilise spaces that might otherwise be wasted. As well as a desk you might also want to include a comfortable chair with good lighting for reading.

Play area: If you do not have the space for a separate playroom for your children you can create a play corner with some good storage that enables the toys to be stored out of sight. Try to position the play area away from the main seating area so that when the toys are packed away you still have a 'grown-up' space for relaxing or entertaining.

Choosing the perfect sofa

▶ The seat depth and back height should allow you to sit comfortably, neither too slumped nor too upright, and to get up easily.

▶ Look for a frame with smooth, well-fitting joints and no knots, splits or cracks. When you sit down it shouldn't 'give' more than a little.

▶ Cushions should be well stuffed, and seams stitched straight and strong.

▶ A washable loose cover is a good idea if you have children or animals.

▶ Don't overcrowd a small room with a huge sofa. But in a large room, a tiny sofa will disappear.

▶ Will it go through your front door? If your hall is exceptionally narrow, look for a model with removable back, arms and/or legs.

Group sofas together to make the most of your space; here, a contrasting box adds surface for books and mugs.

FURNITURE

Whether you choose designer style or second-hand bargains, aim to buy
furniture that is well-made, comfortable and solid. Quality pieces will stand
the test of time and give great value for money.

When we furnish a room, very few of us start from scratch.
Try to include pieces you own, and mix with carefully
chosen items to complete the look.

FURNITURE FOR LIVING

What do you do in your living room? It can be a space
for relaxing, reading, entertaining, playing, crafting, even
working – so you will need to make sure every single
item of furniture works really hard to earn its place.
Comfortable seating is your first priority. A pair of sofas
that face each other, or perhaps L-shaped modular
seating, can be a good-looking and convivial alternative
to the traditional three-piece suite, while a single sofa can
be supplemented with an interesting chair or two, or even
a beanbag or floor cushion. Coffee tables, often seen as
essential, take up lots of floor space and can interrupt the
flow of movement around the room; you may be better
off with side tables, a console table against the back of the
sofa, or even a small chest of drawers at one arm, which
can double up as useful extra storage space.

In small rooms, look for neat, low pieces, but avoid

making everything miniature, or you could end up
with a doll's-house effect. In large rooms, generously
sized, high-backed furnishings work well. Group them
sociably rather than placing them around the edges
of the room, which can look somewhat institutional.
If you are in any doubt as to how to arrange your
furniture, there's a really simple solution: make life-
sized paper templates and lay them out on the floor.
Simply move them around until everything feels as if
it's in its rightful place.

SPACE-SAVING FURNITURE

Sofa bed
Perfect for putting up last-minute guests. Before you buy, make sure both the sofa and the mattress are comfortable and hardwearing, and that the opening mechanism is easy to operate.

Extending dining table
One leaf or two? Round, oval, square or rectangular? Traditional or modern? Choose an extending table to make room for dinner parties or family get-togethers.

Stacking chairs
For when you need extra seating, chairs that can be stacked away when not in use can be really handy. Or how about a set of stools, which can be pushed under the table tidily?

Nesting side tables
In a small living room it's great to be able to 'nest' side tables together so they take up less floor space when you're not actually using them. These days you can find some up-to-date styles.

Coffee table with storage
Coffee tables inevitably get piled with all sorts of things, so it makes sense to choose one with either a drawer or a shelf beneath. Or use a chest and enjoy capacious storage space.

Hideaway desk
A hinged desk that folds down from the wall is an ideal option for occasional admin. Or you could conceal an entire office in a cleverly designed cupboard or bureau.

ADDING VISUAL INTEREST

Living rooms, particularly seating areas, need to have some points of visual
interest so that everyone can relax and feel at ease.

FOCAL POINTS

Traditionally, the fireplace is the chief focal point in a living
room; firelight gives a sense of warmth and well-being.
If you have a fireplace that has been boxed in, it is worth
restoring, and if you don't have a fireplace, it might be
worth considering adding one.

Perhaps not traditionally, but certainly conventionally,
televisions come a close second to providing a focal
point. While most homes have more than one, the
main living room is still a place where people watch
television, and the place that operates as a home media
centre, with computers, DVD players and CD players.
All these items will need to be integrated into the living
room. The television should be situated so that viewing
is comfortable but not be unduly domineering. If it is the
focal point, make sure you choose one that fits in with the
rest of the room.

Windows act as focal points and, if you have a great
view, think hard about how much privacy you need before
you decide to add curtains or blinds. However, you will
need to consider glare, especially when deciding where
to position the television. When choosing a window
treatment, make sure the colour and pattern relates to the
rest of the furniture and flooring in the room.

Walls and ceilings play a large part in any decorative
scheme; use colour or pattern on walls as a focal point.
Paint a wall or maybe a partition in a strong or intense
colour, or use wallpaper, to accentuate the way space is
divided. Colour and pattern on walls can also provide a
backdrop to a specific area within an open-plan living
room. If you are concerned about space, paint ceilings
a few shades lighter than the walls. However, a very tall
ceiling painted in a darker colour will provide visual
interest and an intimate atmosphere.

Once the furniture layout is settled, think about the
lighting in the living room. Mostly it's common sense:
bright lights for reading; pleasing, suitably muted lighting
for watching television and relaxation; and even more
subdued, flattering lighting for parties.

*In this simple scheme, faux-
book wallpaper furnishes the
alcoves while a mirror adds a
focal point.*

MIRRORS

A mirror enhances the effect of natural light and increases the sense of spaciousness. As well as creating the illusion of space, a large mirror on a chimney breast or in an alcove can create a point of interest. If mirrors are placed close to any outside space, they can reflect views inside.

Bevelled mirrors can look uninspiring if hung individually, but a collection of them will give multiple reflections and visual interest. Similarly, you can use various types of mirrors with a variety of frames in conjunction with other artwork.

DISPLAYS

The way you display a collection is almost as important as the objects themselves. Collections can take pride of place, say on shelving in alcoves; equally, a slightly isolated position works well (see Halls, stairs and landings, pages 118–119). Either way, a display can be a very interesting visual point of reference. A glass cabinet will confine your collection so that it doesn't spread and take over.

Tables can be used for displays: a low table with an arrangement of, for instance, small lacquer boxes or other objects, can also become a focal point in a living room. Use your imagination, you may come up with quirky alternatives that are a visible reflection of your own interests.

A collection of artwork – paintings, prints or photographs – is one of the most popular forms of display and can offer stunning visual interest.

Tiles have been used to create a large mirror to reflect light and colour around this striking room.

This symmetrical display of book pages framed in black is highly effective.

TECHNOLOGY

Love it or hate it, we can't live without technology.
Make the most of it or hide it away – it's your decision.

There is no getting away from the fact that the TV is nearly always the focal point of a modern living room. But it doesn't have to dominate. Avoid purpose-built stands as they are rarely very attractive – you are better off with a side table, low cupboard or shelf that suits the overall style of the room. And it's easy to mount a TV on a swing-arm support or pop it on a wheeled trolley, so you can push it out of sight whenever you wish.

Alternatively, upcycle an old cabinet into an all-purpose media unit (drill holes in the back for leads and to avoid heat build-up) and you can simply shut the doors when the set is off.

Flat screen TVs are much easier to disguise than old-fashioned, deep-backed ones. Mounted on the wall, they can even become part of the artwork.

Chargers are probably the biggest bugbear of the modern home. For organisation's sake, keep them all in one place – a drawer near a socket is neat and efficient. Or consider buying a single charging station that all your gadgets can sit on. There are all sorts of stands, fasteners, tidies and other inexpensive accessories that are no end of help when it comes to organising techno-jumble; then again, it is possible to do a neat job of it with handwritten labels and wire ties. If your remote control is always getting lost, just stick on some hook-and-loop tape so you can attach it to the side of the TV.

Cupboards or shelves can be used as media units to store or hide away satellite boxes and games consoles.

In large rooms you can combine a variety of different wall coverings to great effect. This room combines a dark feature wall with painted wooden panelling and elegant stripes.

Capitalise on high ceilings by using a small area of wall to create a large amount of storage.

Attention to detail and a cohesive colour scheme ensure that this mid-century modern scheme works well in the living room of this Victorian building.

In this scheme, neutral walls show off dark wood and leather furniture to their best advantage; the coloured tiles in the fireplace are echoed in the cushions and the unusual light fitting.

Living rooms / 135

Fitted window seats are a brilliant use of space in a bay window, and the wealth of cushions makes the room feel colourful and cosy.

Carefully positioned mirrors will reflect light around rooms that might otherwise feel dark.

An elaborate chandelier and a pair of antique chairs complement this imposing stone fireplace perfectly.

A bay window provides a perfect place for additional living room seating; heavy curtains add luxury and will keep out draughts in cold weather.

DINING ROOMS

While some people believe that dining rooms are outdated, others are embracing the fact it is useful to have a separate dining room that can also be used for other purposes.

Eating habits have changed enormously over the past 20 years. Everyone's time is at a premium, not many people cook elaborate meals; it is quite tempting and very easy to buy a ready-meal or have a take-away. In addition, a kitchen is no longer purely functional – it tends to be the heart of the home or part of 'the family room', where people eat, live and entertain. Basically, lifestyles are less formal than they used to be. These changes have played a role in the demise of the dining room, as have television renovation programmes, which regularly suggest that open-plan spaces have the wow factor. As a consequence, in many homes the dining room is the first room to be sacrificed in order to create a kitchen/dining room or living/dining room.

Formal dining rooms can still found in large houses or luxurious high-end properties, where space (and money) are not an issue.

In this dining room the table has been replaced with a snooker table with a custom-made cover that can be folded back.

Tips for creating a multi-purpose dining room

► Keep the room alive by using the table for piles of books that can easily moved. Alternatively, line the walls with books to create a library.
► Use as an occasional office, with space for the computer and papers to be tidied away when you eat. Children can also do their homework here.
► Think about a games room – a large dining table can double up as a table tennis or pool table.
► Extendable tables are a good idea, allowing you to cater for different numbers of people and giving you extra space if you are using the room for other purposes.
► Flexible dining rooms can be dressed up for entertaining, or down during the day.

The debate about whether or not we are seeing the demise of the dining room is ongoing. Supporters of the dining room have excellent points to make, which definitely provide food for thought. For a start, having a kitchen and a dining room allows for separate cooking and eating areas, preventing cooking smells, steam and noise to permeate the dining area. Similarly, dining rooms allow adults to talk or listen to music in one room while children play, do their homework or watch television in another. Dining rooms work well when the space relates to other rooms in the house, and if you're prepared to be adaptable, a dining room could become one of the most useful rooms in the house.

Create a bold statement and bring your dining room furniture back to life using paint effects.

Mismatched or different-coloured chairs can also add variety to a dining room.

FURNITURE

Whether you have a separate dining room, or your dining area is part of your kitchen or open-plan living space, meals should be enjoyed in a comfortable, relaxed atmosphere.

The dining table is a focal point for lots of activities, for doing homework, playing games, conversation and, above all, for the pleasure of eating – everyday family meals and cosy suppers for guests. The table is the centre of any eating space, and there should be ample room to move around when serving a meal. But for the rest of the time you may want to position it to the side of a room or even against a wall. It can be moved when necessary, to accommodate guests.

CHOOSING A DINING TABLE

Dining tables come in all shapes and sizes, so where to begin? The choice of table will be determined by the space available, the number of people it has to accommodate and, of course, the style of your home.

Round tables will seat more people comfortably than rectangular tables, and are generally considered to be more sociable. There is no head of the table and everyone can see each other easily. Obviously, if you need to place a table alongside a wall, a rectangular table is a better option. And where space is at a premium, you might want to use a small table, again, probably rectangular, that fits into a recess or bay window; extra leaves can extend square and rectangular tables.

If the table is going to be used for different purposes, the surface will need to be durable, so polished wood is probably not a good option, although you can always use a protective tablecloth. Washable surfaces are important for relaxed meal times with children.

Wooden tables are the most popular, whatever their style, and if they are solid wood they will be extremely hardwearing. Glass tables can complement a modern room, and help make the room look spacious, because you can see through them, but if you have children you may worry that they could run into the table, or even that something could be dropped on it, causing it to break.

Apart from wood and glass, dining tables come in a wide range of materials, such as veneered wood,

melamine foil finishes, chrome-plated steel and glass and painted wood. As with the shape and size, choose the material from both a utilitarian and style point of view.

An antique, vintage or second-hand table is worth considering, especially if it fits in with the rest of the room. They can be bought from antique or second-hand shops, online auction sites, and through auction houses. Very often this is an economical way of buying a dining table; a solid wood, brand-new table will be much more expensive.

In today's less formal society, matching sets of dining chairs are no longer de rigeur – you can combine contemporary chairs with a vintage table or vice versa. The main thing is to choose chairs that are comfortable; there should be plenty of room for knees between the seat and the table.

DINING ROOM STORAGE

Cutlery, glass and china is often stored in the kitchen for ease of use; it can be washed up and put straight away. However, you may need storage in the dining room/area for extra china, glasses, mats and table linen. Sideboards, the traditional way of storing dining room accessories, are making a comeback. As well as offering good storage, they provide a useful surface for plates, serving dishes, water jugs, wine and so on. If space is tight, narrow, built-in cupboards might be a better option. These could be fitted either side of a chimney breast or along a wall.

Painted wooden furniture will give your dining room a fresh, Scandinavian feel.

Glass-fronted storage is perfect for displaying your china and glassware.

Before you buy checklist

▶ How do you envisage your ideal eating area?
▶ How many people usually eat at the table?
▶ How often will it be used and for how long?
▶ Is the table going to be in a self-contained space?
▶ Is it going to be used for other purposes?
▶ Will it be subjected to a great deal of wear and tear?
▶ What is your budget?

DINING ROOM DÉCOR

In order to create a relaxed, comfortable eating area, carefully combine wall and window treatments, and lighting.

Separate dining rooms are mostly used in the evenings, for special occasions and for entertaining. Consequently, they offer great scope for decoration; this is one room where you can get a little carried away. Warm, dark shades work well and provide a cosy atmosphere, and are often chosen because they look good in artificial light – glass and silver on the table glitters in sharp contrast. Red is traditionally associated with dining rooms, but you could combine bold colour choices with contemporary boxy bookcases and keep other elements, such as curtains, more neutral for a modern twist. This is not to say that a dining room can't be bright, airy and full of sunshine, especially if there are French doors that open out onto a garden. A lovely wallpaper design can be used to good effect in dining rooms, adding colour, pattern and texture.

Whatever the shape and location of your dining area, the décor should reflect your lifestyle. For example, if you eat in a kitchen/dining room, and you like giving dinner parties, use an informal colour scheme, maybe choosing two complimentary colours in each area. Be flexible,

think about how you can transform the dining area in the evening. Use mirrors, not only to maximise light, but also to add a touch of sparkle when reflecting cutlery and glassware from the tabletop.

If you are painting the walls with a bold colour then the window treatment should tie in or complement the rest of the scheme. Lined curtains or blinds in a dining room will help with the acoustics – an important yet often overlooked element; easy conversation is key to any gathering around the dining table.

Lighting is an essential factor in defining spaces and creating mood; use lighting to help put your dining table in focus. A strong central light over the table can look stunning, but the height is crucial – it must not glare in people's eyes. Keep other light sources subdued for maximum effect – dimmer switches will help. Experiment with the level of lighting to achieve the perfect balance. And remember, when you are entertaining, there is nothing quite like low-tech, soft, flattering candlelight.

DINING ROOMS AND OFFICES

If your office forms part of your dining room your office furniture will
need to fit in with the rest of your design scheme.

A STYLISH STUDY

When working from home,
personality is as important as
efficiency so, provided they are
practical, why not look for more
interesting alternatives such as
old school lockers, a blackboard
resting on a pair of metal filing
cabinets, an architect's plan chest
or a distressed kitchen dresser? And
while it is a good idea to choose a
chair on wheels that swivels and is
height-adjustable, it doesn't have
to be boring black – it could be
upholstered in a joyful pattern
that will enhance your office.
Hunt around auctions, junk shops,
markets and the like for home office
furniture that you actually find
appealing. As long as it's in good
condition and suits the space, there
are no limits on style.

*Traditional writing desks are
beautiful pieces of furniture
as well as being a useful
addition to any family space.*

Fabric chair covers are a quick way to update furniture and give a room a whole new look.

Use built-in shelving in dining rooms to create a library area or provide an interesting display.

Dining room tables and chairs do not need to match; you can mix different styles of chairs or mix chairs and benches.

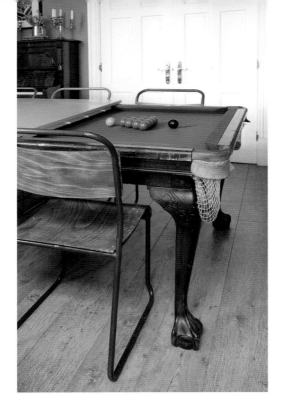

In this dining room the table has been replaced with a snooker table with a custom-made cover that can be folded back.

Add colour and interest to a large table with a simple row of plants.

Lined curtains or blinds in a dining room will help with the acoustics when entertaining; always make sure the window treatments complement the rest of the scheme.

KITCHENS

What makes a good-looking, functional kitchen – where you can cook, eat and spend time together as a family? Careful planning is the answer.

First, assess exactly what you need from the kitchen. Ask yourself lots of questions. Who will use it and how often? How will it be used – for regular family meals or the occasional microwave dinner? And what about other activities – homework, watching TV, doing the washing or ironing? Do you have lots of kitchen gadgets and will you keep them on worktops or in cupboards? Do you prefer solid or glass-fronted cupboards, or lots of open shelves? Will you have some unfitted elements, such as a dresser or sideboard? Would you prefer built-in or freestanding appliances? What about worktops, sinks and flooring? Next, do plenty of research, and visit every showroom within reach. Consider what styles you like, and what you can afford. Ultimately, it's best to avoid fashion fads; invest in quality and, above all, go with what feels right for you.

HOW TO PLAN A KITCHEN

Deciding where the sink will go is often a good place to start when designing a kitchen. From there, it is usually best to place the main food preparation area between the sink and the hob, ensuring that this worktop space is large enough to serve up a meal, and has enough power points nearby for small appliances. Depending on your hob/cooker, it may need to go against an exterior wall or chimney, and it should certainly be sited so that hot pans can be carried to the sink easily. Place the fridge at the end of a run of cupboards. Remember to allow enough space around your appliances to open doors comfortably. Experts recommend a 'work triangle' between the cooker, sink and fridge. This may not work for you, but aim to leave an uninterrupted space between the areas you use the most.

KITCHEN LAYOUTS

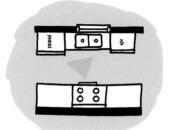

Single line

The only option if your kitchen is along one wall. Place the sink between the fridge and hob, and try to maximise the length of work surface, fitting built-in appliances below and wall units above.

Galley

In a narrow kitchen you can fit a line of units and appliances along each side. When well-designed, this can be extremely convenient, though it is best for a one- or two-person home.

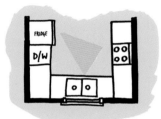

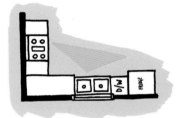

U-shaped

A U-shape gives plenty of storage and working space, but only possible if you have stretches of wall on three sides. In a large room, be wary of having to walk too far from one side to the other.

L-shaped

This layout is useful in a square or rectangular kitchen if you need space for a table, and if two people are using the kitchen at the same time. Plan the corner carefully to avoid a clash of doors.

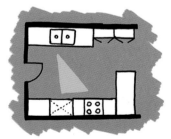

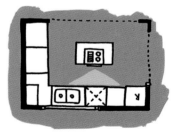

Peninsula

Add a unit at right angles to one end of a U- or L-shaped kitchen, and you have a peninsula. Very handy as a breakfast bar or extra work surface that can be accessed from both sides.

Island

An island gives extra storage and workspace as well as an eating area. Don't make it so big you can't reach the middle, and plan the room so that you are not constantly walking round it.

KITCHEN CUPBOARDS

From the most traditional, solid-wood, Shaker-style kitchen unit to the glossiest of flat-fronted, lacquered modern versions, there really are endless styles of kitchen cupboard to choose from.

Colour, finish and style are not your only choices. Do you want units that are machine-made or individually constructed by hand? Budget will probably help you decide, and it's worth bearing in mind that machine-made units are not necessarily poor quality, though they will have 'plant-on' doors that sit in front of the frame, rather than 'in-frame' doors, which have to be individually made.

If you want to avoid the bland, box-like look of the conventional fitted kitchen, vary things by specifying wall cupboards of different heights or colours, or replacing some solid cupboard doors with glass fronts. For a more open look, opt for base units on legs rather than those hidden by plinths, replace wall units with shelves, hooks and racks, and create interesting displays of your crockery, glassware and attractively packaged food.

FITTING YOUR KITCHEN

When buying a fitted kitchen, ensure that you are clear on who will install it – does the company have a team of experienced fitters, or will you have to find someone yourself? If you are buying a flatpack, are you confident in your own abilities to put it together? Just remember: a good fitter can make an average kitchen look amazing,

Update your kitchen cupboards

1 Remove the doors and drawer fronts and take off the handles, hinges and any other hardware.

2 Thoroughly sand everything you plan to paint or stain.

3 Mask the areas on the insides of the carcasses that you don't want to paint.

4 Carefully apply a suitable primer, undercoat and topcoat, or a wood stain.

5 Replace any hinges that are worn or not working properly and, if necessary, change the knobs or handles, too (you may need to fill holes if they don't match the existing ones).

while poor fitting can make even an expensive kitchen look terrible.

UNFITTED KITCHENS

Fitted kitchens are the norm these days, but you can still add one or two freestanding pieces to create a charming, informal look – or even create an entire kitchen from assorted cupboards, tables, dressers and shelves. The trick to mixing and matching successfully is to plan in advance, ensuring that adjacent pieces are very similar in depth and height, that wall units and shelves are aligned in order to create visual coherence, and that you have a pleasing blend of materials, colours and finishes.

Worktop-to-ceiling, glass-fronted cupboards will provide all the kitchen storage you need.

These pale blue, Shaker-style cupboards are a perfect mix of modern and traditional.

WORKTOPS

Worktops and splashbacks can dramatically alter the character of a kitchen.
As well as looking good, they must be tough and durable, too.

First things first, worktops must be easy to clean, without nooks and crannies that can harbour germs. They must be tough enough to withstand wear and tear, and resistant to knives, heat, steam and water. Splashbacks and upstands (their smaller cousins) should be smooth, wipeable, waterproof and durable enough to protect the walls behind your sink and hob. Because every material has its own, unique qualities, your best option may be to fit different surfaces in different areas of your kitchen.

Having considered the practicalities, next comes the fun part. There are endless choices of material, colour and finish for both worktops and splashbacks. Most materials can be used for both surfaces (usually cut thinner when used vertically), so you can opt for a seamless, all-over look, or mix and match for an interesting effect. You can choose a surface that will blend into the background, or create a look-at-me, wow-factor feature. You may prefer natural colours or dramatic, vibrant shades. One thing is certain: whatever your style, there's a surface to suit you.

Wooden worktops have a classic look but need to be sealed regularly to keep them in good condition.

TYPES OF WORKTOP

Stone
Granite is the toughest option. Slate, limestone and marble are more porous and need treating with a specialist sealant.

Stone composites
Made using a mixture of crushed quartz and a bonding agent, composites are strong and non-porous.

Timber
An elegant, warm and timeless option, but it does need regular sealing. End-grain hardwood makes a good inset cutting area.

Bamboo
With a distinctive grain, bamboo is hard-wearing. It can be sanded just like timber, but needs regular maintenance.

Concrete
This comes in a range of colours and finishes. Heat- and stain-resistant, hard-wearing and waterproof when sealed.

Laminates
Usually a less expensive option and available in many colours and patterns, some of which mimic natural surfaces.

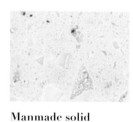

Manmade solid surfaces
These are made from a mix of acrylic resin and minerals. Stain-resistant, non-porous, easy to clean and durable.

Metal
Stainless steel is hygienic, heatproof, waterproof and hard-wearing. Thick steel is recommended for durability.

Glass
Glass surfaces come in a range of colours, and are heat-resistant, easy to clean and totally waterproof. Scratches are a risk.

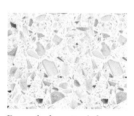

Recycled materials
Options include recycled glass, plastic and industrial and consumer waste.

SINKS, TAPS AND HOODS

A good-looking sink fitted with beautiful taps is often the focal point of a kitchen. And don't forget the cooker hood – as well as a practical necessity, it can be a decorative enhancement to your scheme.

SELECTING A SINK

Kitchen sinks come in all sorts of shapes, sizes, colours and materials – your ideal choice is a sink that has the ability to withstand hard usage as well as good looks that complement your other fixtures, materials and general colour scheme.

Choose from stainless steel, ceramic, composite stone or even timber, copper or concrete. Sinks can be undermounted, inset, farmhouse-style or even moulded from the same material as the worktop. As for size, you may opt for a compact or corner sink to suit a tiny space, a one-and-a-half bowl version with a drainer that means

you can wash up and rinse at the same time, or an oversized sink to cope with large pans and utensils.

TYPES OF TAPS

Choose a tap that suits the style and size of your kitchen and works with your water pressure. Check that it is high enough to get your pans under, and reaches properly over the sink. For best quality, look for a solid metal body with ceramic discs in the cartridge. A handy option is a pull-out spray tap that lets you rinse your washing up quickly and easily.

- **Pillar:** This has two taps, one hot, one cold, with cross-head or lever handles.
- **Monobloc:** One tap mixes hot and cold water, controlled via one or two handles or levers.
- **Wall-mounted:** A tap that frees up space and makes cleaning easier.
- **Pull-out:** Features an extendable spray hose.
- **Swivel:** An essential tap for reaching both bowls of a double sink.
- **Water filter:** Add a water filter to reduce impurities in your water.
- **Boiling water:** This tap provides boiling water instantly (there are safety features built in).
- **Colour-changing:** An LED light ring illuminates the water.

A matt black monobloc tap contrasts well with a chrome sink.

This stainless steel cooker hood gives a modern touch.

A kitchen on a budget?

- When comparing prices, check exactly what's included: design and planning, disposal of existing fittings, plumbing and electrical work, associated building work, fitting flooring, tiling, carpentry? Is there a guarantee or after-sales service?
- Veneered doors are usually cheaper than solid wood. Chipboard carcasses are cheapest – but look for at least 18–20mm (¾in) thick.
- Avoid thin metal hinges, which can wear quickly.
- High-pressure laminate worktops are more durable than low-pressure ones.
- Don't skimp on fitting. A good fitter can make a distinctly average kitchen appear fantastic, whereas poor fitting will make the most luxurious kitchen look terrible.

COOKER HOODS

A cooker hood is essential to get rid of steam and smells. There are two types: those which extract, via ducting, to the outside of your house, and those that filter out odours and smoke, then recirculate the clean air back into your kitchen. Before you buy, you'll need to know the extraction rate – ideally 12 times an hour – and check how noisy the extractor is when it's switched on. There are all sorts of style options, from totally concealed, integrated hoods to statement-making versions that double up as stunning light fittings.

KITCHEN-DINER

The current trend is for kitchens to serve as informal living spaces where people can sit and enjoy their meals together, adding to the enjoyment of life.

In a kitchen-diner, the person who is preparing the food or cooking can socialise with family or friends at the same time, and he or she is not isolated, or toiling away while others relax.

Kitchen-diners have two key functions: cooking and eating. If you are planning from scratch, always place the eating zone near a window or French (bi-fold or sliding) doors, where there is natural light. This will allow you to open the windows and doors on a sunny day, provide views of any outside space, and let the outside in while you are sat around the dining table. The kitchen zone can afford to be in the darker area as you can cook under artificial light.

If you have a long rectangular room, place the kitchen units halfway down both sides, as opposed to all the way along one side, then both areas can be used independently. For extra storage, you can always add a freestanding piece of furniture.

In a self-contained kitchen, you will need to create a dining area in the living area. When the kitchen is visible from the dining area, try to screen appliances and preparation areas as far as possible. Dimmer switches help to vary the focus of attention in the evening.

While it's good to differentiate between the two functions, bear in mind that a kitchen-diner is still one room, so remember to think of the design as a whole.

BREAKFAST BARS

In spacious kitchens, state-of-the-art breakfast bars can be added to equally 'on trend' island units. They serve many functions and provide an extra surface for entertaining: while the host is busy cooking, guests can be having a pre-dinner drink at the bar. They can also be used for informal meals, and especially – as the name suggests – for breakfast, when most people don't have time to linger at the dining table.

In small kitchens, breakfast bars are a godsend, they needn't take up much space; a narrow counter can be fitted along one wall, made from the same worktop as is used in the kitchen, or from wood to add contrast.

Whatever the size of your kitchen, breakfast bars can also be fitted in a U-shaped layout, a peninsula or room divider (half height), with cupboards and appliances on the other side.

FOLD-AWAY TABLES

If you are short of space you may not have room for a dining table and chairs. One solution is a fold-away or fold-down table, which makes the most of limited space, and makes it possible to eat in the kitchen. There are some ingenious designs available, including ones that slide out from under the worktop. Generally, though, they will only seat two to three people, but they can be useful when you need to grab a quick bite, and for informal meals.

KITCHEN APPLIANCES

Cookers, ovens, hobs and white goods form the engine of the kitchen.
What you choose needs careful consideration in order to make preparing
food both enjoyable and efficient.

With a mind-boggling array of products – cookers, refrigerators, dishwashers, washing machines and tumble dryers – to choose from, it's a challenge to figure out what is right for you. Budget will help you to prioritise, but it's best to choose good-quality products that suit your lifestyle. For instance, unless you're always entertaining and catering for large numbers, don't be tempted by a huge, multi-function double oven or range. This goes for refrigerators, too: ask yourself whether an American-style refrigerator, which takes up a lot of room and can be costly to run, is right for you; or will a low-level, integrated fridge and freezer better suit your layout.

COOKERS

Although there are masses to choose from, basically, there are two main types – freestanding cookers (stoves) or separate ovens (built under or at eye-level) with hobs fitted into the worktop. Of course you can have gas burners, electric hotplates, ceramic tops and induction hobs, in a wide range of combinations. Cookers, too, can be powered by gas or electricity, or a combination of both – an electric oven and gas rings – often deemed to be the optimum choice. However, in some locations gas is not available, so this will have to be considered. Base your decision about what cooker to buy on the following criteria: the amount of space you have, what will look good, and what will suit your requirements and your budget.

WHITE GOODS

Integrated appliances are a good choice because they help to blur the line between kitchen and dining areas. This streamlined option is especially true if you have to accommodate all four of the major white goods – washing machine, dishwasher, refrigerator and freezer – in the kitchen. If you are lucky enough to have a utility area where the laundry is done, then it's not so crucial and you could just have an integrated dishwasher. Integrated refrigerators, freezers or fridge-freezers can be built under the worksurface or at eye-level.

Freestanding fridge-freezers in stainless steel or gleaming enamel can make a statement in your kitchen, if you have the space. You can even have a side-by-side wine cooler and fridge-freezer providing excellent storage for everything from Sauvignon Blanc to sorbet.

Extractor hoods are available in some interesting and quirky designs.

HEAT, LIGHT AND VENTILATION

The kitchen is the only room in the house that produces its own heat: from cooking appliances and, to a lesser extent, refrigerators and freezers. It is also susceptible to the problem of condensation. An extractor fan is a good solution as it can produce significant drops in temperature and is an efficient means of expelling moisture.

It's worth investing in a good extractor hood over the cooker/hob, particularly in kitchen-diners, or open-plan living spaces, to eliminate odours, grease and steam. The latest models are quiet with efficient lighting built in.

However, the more streamlined they are, the easier they are to keep clean.

Conventional radiators are not appropriate in kitchens as they often waste valuable wall space, although they can be fitted in dining areas – underfloor heating works well.

When it comes to light in the kitchen, it is essential to have general and specific lighting. Around work surfaces, sinks and ovens and hobs you will need bright light. Integrated lights under wall units are a good idea – mini fluorescent strips don't get hot, and send a diffused, warm light onto surfaces below.

*A simple wall unit can
provide both shelving
and hanging space.*

*Island units provide an
additional work surface
and can also be used as
a breakfast bar or for
entertaining.*

*Incorporate fireplaces
into your kitchen design
by using the mantelpiece
to provide additional
storage.*

In small kitchens white units will make the room feel bigger; make use of as much wall space as you can with a combination of shelves and hooks.

This U-shaped kitchen incorporates a breakfast bar; a piece of wire between the wall and the worktop provides a place to hang artwork.

This kitchen is clean, white and modern but the wooden worktop makes the room feel warmer and matches the flooring.

You can mix and match fitted drawers and cupboards with freestanding units and shelves to create a kitchen that is completely individual.

In a kitchen-diner always site the eating area next to a window or French doors where there is natural light.

This kitchen combines different types of freestanding units in a variety of finishes to give a rustic, French-style look.

WORK AREAS

Whatever the activity or task, it will always feel easier and more pleasurable
in a stimulating, well-organised area.

Lifestyle changes have had an effect on how, where and
when we work. Working from home is an increasingly
viable option for many people due to sophisticated
communication systems, as well as relatively inexpensive
computer and office equipment. If you can take over
a whole room, then you won't have to worry about
your office fitting in with other elements in the design
scheme, something that will be necessary if you have to
accommodate your office space in another room.

If you are working from home every day, your office
should be furnished and equipped so that you can work
efficiently and productively. Working at a desk continually
can cause problems – back pain, repetitive strain injury
(RSI) and eye strain. Choose ergonomically designed
furniture; make sure that your desk is the right height and
your chair has been designed for office use.

For more general use, whatever space you have for your
home office – perhaps even a dual-purpose dining room/
study – flexible organisation is the key to success. It needs
to be carefully thought through in every detail to create
stimulating surroundings.

SELF-CONTAINED OFFICE

Mix business and pleasure with the latest furniture
and equipment for your office at home. Apart from
essential equipment – seating, a desk with a solid
work surface, good basic equipment and glare-free
lighting – be creative with storage. You could mix
industrial-type shelving with metal cupboards, or a
traditional oak desk with library shelves. A piece of
designer furniture can add instant style to a functional

space. For anyone who has occasional meetings, a large table can be used as a flexible desk, as it can be pulled out from the wall. A wooden slatted blind is useful in an office as it can shade the room on a sunny day, or be pulled up completely when you need more natural light.

MULTI-FUNCTIONAL SPACES

There are lots of possibilities for delineating a workspace in other areas, even if you only have a corner of a room to house a computer and a desk. Partitions, screens (freestanding and fitted) and storage units can be used to divide work and living areas. Some screens will slide so that the office can be masked completely. In dual-purpose rooms or small-space offices, organise the space and store equipment without compromising either work or living activities; you need to be able to clear away the office when not in use. The simpler the design, the quicker the transition from workspace to living space, and vice versa.

If you mainly require a workstation, the key decision is where to site it. Think about putting it near or in front of a window in a living area or bedroom; it may aid concentration. Make use of odd space – on a generous-sized landing or under the stairs. Build your workstation into a wall of storage, including a fold-down or pull-out desk, with shelves above. If you have a very high ceiling you could even consider a platform level, provided head height is sufficient.

This office combines elements of modern and retro design with a glass-topped desk and a vintage chair.

Folding chairs and a desk on castors mean that a workspace can be as flexible as possible.

Floating shelves are a great way to store equipment, provided your sockets are close enough to avoid trailing wires.

Setting up a home office

▶ List how many things you need to plug in, and work out how many sockets you will need (you'll probably be surprised). Fix several sockets about three inches above your work surface, and have a few hidden lower down, too.

▶ Organise all your electrical items together – so you don't end up with long cables between them.

▶ For a desk in the middle of the room, you will need floor sockets.

▶ Adjustable wall lamps above your working area free up desk space.

▶ Get ergonomic: site your computer monitor straight ahead of you, about an arm's length away; feet should be flat on the floor, with thighs parallel to the floor; your desk should be about elbow height; when typing, your fingers should be lower than your wrists.

UTILITY ROOMS

A utility room is a useful space, not just for the laundry but also for doing other jobs around the house and garden. If you haven't got one, it's worth considering creating a utility area in a little-used space.

A dedicated laundry/utility room frees up living space. Ideally it should house a sink, washing machine, dryer and ironing board, as well as cleaning utensils, mops, vacuum cleaners and other household necessities. A butler's sink is particularly useful for hand washing, soaking, bleaching or washing bulky items. Some sort of counter next to the sink allows you to sort clothes prior to and after washing; and a drying rack is also handy when tumble dryers can't be used.

New-builds – houses and flats – often have laundry equipment (washing machine and tumble dryer) situated in a separate utility area away from the kitchen. This makes a great deal of sense in any home but particularly those with open-plan designs or kitchen/dining rooms. It not only provides more space in the kitchen, but also reduces noise from the washing machine, and the washing itself doesn't have to be sorted and on view when you're about to eat a meal.

In utility rooms, flooring needs to be durable and able to stand up to possible soaking. Walls should be painted in washable paint, which is stain- and scuff- resistant.

Many essential but messy tasks can be done in the utility room, out of the way of easily damaged surfaces. It is also a good location for boilers, freezers and meters.

Wall-mounted hangers are a great, space-saving way to dry laundry on a wet day without having to hang it around the house.

Recycling takes a bit of effort and boxes or bins can take up a lot of space, but creating an organised section in your utility area will make the job a lot easier.

OTHER SPACES AND USES

With careful planning you can make better use of your existing space. A corner of a garage can be transformed into a laundry, complete with plenty of storage for washing products. A utility area doesn't need to have great head height, so think about the possibility of siting one under the stairs, or in a basement/cellar, as long as it's not damp and there's good ventilation. Sometimes you can even fit a washing machine, dryer, airer and shelving into a large cupboard, for instance, off the hall, or in an old larder.

Depending on the size, a utility room can also be used for other purposes. If you are keen on DIY it could double-up as a workroom – somewhere to store tools and materials, keep a portable workbench and a large dustsheet. Alternatively, you might want a hobby room for craft/art materials or a sewing room.

A downstairs loo is very useful in a family home and can be accommodated in a utility room (or vice versa for that matter). It could be screened off from the laundry area or integrated into the design of the room. There are space-saving loos that fit into corners, and the great advantage is that plumbing should not cause too much of a problem.

A utility area in your house means that you have a dedicated space for washing and other essential but messy tasks.

This small multi-functional space has to work very hard. A shelf has been fitted into an alcove to provide space for a computer, and the desk chair can also be used for eating at the table.

A fold-down table, an Eames-style chair and brightly coloured lamp create the perfect office space in this mid-century modern living room.

Places that might not otherwise be used can be made into office areas, such as alcoves, landings and spaces under the stairs.

The fabric for this desk chair has been carefully chosen to complement a Regency-style living room.

BEDROOMS

Decoratively, bedrooms should be restful, welcoming and, above all, personal
havens. Choose a style that works best for you, that suits the structure of
your room, and include elements that will make you happy.

FINDING YOUR STYLE

Bear in mind that your bedroom can be anything you
want it to be. If you're struggling to decide what style
you're after, think about which words convey the feeling
you want to experience in the room. For instance, 'light,
elegant and welcoming' or 'dark, intimate and romantic',
then gather visual samples to meet these criteria. Keep
your influences as broad as possible, but bear in mind
it could be just one item that inspires you or that you
particularly like – anything from a stunning, designer duvet
cover to a vintage dressing table.

When deciding on a scheme, you may have to
incorporate some existing furniture. Once you have settled
on a style, why not upcycle a favourite piece, or an online
auction bargain, to fit in with the new decoration. The
results can be very successful and will give the item a new
lease of life (see page 219).

IDEAS

▶ Choose a theme – a unifying device – such as stripes in
different widths, colour and direction.
▶ Add extra seating to store shoes on, to sit on while
reading, etc. – it could be a bedroom chair or a
storage chest.
▶ Banish television from the bedroom; the bedroom is
about sleeping, it will keep your mind buzzing longer

before you are able to go to sleep. Plus you'll have more room for furniture and accessories.

- Add a collection or display of things you love in the bedroom – make sure you can see them from the bed.
- Try to include some drama into your scheme, or an element of glamour. It could be a theatrical chandelier or just a dark feature wall. Stick with one or two dramatic elements so as not to overdo it.
- Colour and pattern are important; take inspiration from a favourite painting. For a relaxing room, soft colours will work best, from warm light tones to earthy hues. Different shades of white reflect the light and provide a good backdrop for brightly patterned fabric.
- Ceilings deserve attention in a bedroom. Where you have no cornicing, consider wallpapering the ceiling in a pattern to suit your style. If you have a picture rail you could bring the paper down to meet the rail and paint it in a matching colour.

- Ideally, bedroom windows should be double-glazed not only for extra warmth, but also for peace and quiet. If you choose curtains, use blackout interlining, for insulation and darkness.
- Fitted carpet is an obvious choice for floors, but it needn't be expensive as it will not be subject to a great deal of wear. Wooden flooring or painted floorboards can look great; just add a soft, comforting rug at each side of the bed to step out on.

FURNITURE

Invest in quality pieces for the bedroom: a great mattress and spacious wardrobes. For kids, function comes first, but have fun, too.

A PEACEFUL SANCTUARY

A comfortable bed and all-encompassing storage are the key components of a bedroom and, from subtle pieces to statement designs; there are all sorts of options to suit any budget. Flat-packs are cheap and can easily be painted and given new handles for a more upmarket appearance (just make sure they're not too flimsy). Second-hand items from junk shops or auctions can be a solid, handsome choice, too. Don't be afraid to make furniture more useful by screwing in hooks, adding shelves or gluing a mirror onto the back of a door.

A comfortable bed is the most important piece of furniture in the bedroom – and a focal point for decoration.

Bespoke cabin beds are on most kids' wishlists; this one provides a cool hideaway.

Rich colours and fun features like invisible shelves make a girl's room feel grown up.

CHILD'S PLAY

In a child's bedroom, forget themed furniture and choose well-made, simple pieces that will still be useable (even if they have to be given a lick of paint) in decades to come. For younger children, keep furniture around the edges of the room, leaving plenty of play space in the middle. As for teenagers, a homework area is important, as is a chill-out zone with a relaxing chair or beanbag. Add a dressing table (this could double up as the desk), a mirror and, for good organisation, a pin board or magnetic board and some open-topped storage for all those bits and pieces that you'd prefer not to end up on the floor.

A good night's sleep

- ▶ Choose as big a bed as you can. Disturbance from a partner (or children) is one of the most common causes of sleeping complaints.
- ▶ The mattress should be comfortable and supportive. Lying down, slide the flat of your hand into the hollow of your back. If it slides in very easily, the bed is too firm; if it's hard to slide your hand in, the bed is too soft.
- ▶ If you and your partner prefer different mattresses, or are very different in weight, you may need a combination mattress, or two singles that zip together.
- ▶ Launder pillows regularly and replace every few years.

WARDROBES

In a bedroom, after the bed, wardrobes are the second most important piece
of furniture, so it's important to find one that best suits your needs.

WARDROBES

Before choosing a wardrobe it's a good idea to edit your
clothes; it's estimated that we wear only 20% of the clothes
we own, which means a huge 80% of the space allocated
for clothes storage is wasted space. Once you have
cleared out your wardrobe, you can decide on exactly
how much storage space you will need.

As with every other room in the house, careful planning
is essential. Work out how much hanging and drawer or
shelf space you will need. Think about the height of the
rail – do you need one placed high enough to take coats
and long dresses? Or would two at half height be suitable
as it would double the amount of hanging space? Also
consider whether you need space for other items – shoes,
bags and accessories.

Wardrobe doors and finishes

- **Sliding:** An optimum choice for bedrooms with
  limited space.
- **Mirror:** Adds glamour and elegance and is space
  enhancing.
- **Translucent glass:** Lightens the look of built-in
  storage, especially when backlit.
- **Coloured high gloss:** Use if you want to inject
  some vibrant colour into your room.
- **Panelled:** For a traditional or Shaker-style
  bedroom.
- **Off-white:** A hardworking wardrobe that will fit
  into most schemes.
- **Wooden:** These can be painted to blend in with
  the rest of the room.

FREESTANDING WARDROBES

Generally, a freestanding wardrobe is more versatile and will give your bedroom a more relaxed feel than a fitted version, which is more streamlined. For a start, if you want a change of layout, a freestanding wardrobe can be moved to a different position. Built-in storage does not suit every room, and you may just prefer the look of a traditional wardrobe, or it may be better suited to the style or size of your room. For instance, if you have limited space, you may only have room for a single wardrobe, or one that is narrower than usual.

Freestanding wardrobes come in a wide variety of sizes and styles; they can be bought on the high street or from specialist shops, and can be handmade, antique, vintage or second-hand.

BUILT-IN WARDROBES

If you want to make the most of your space, it's advisable to go for built-in storage because it's less visually intrusive and more spatially efficient. Options include various mass-market types, specialist wardrobe systems that can be tailored to your requirements, and bespoke versions that are made to your specifications. All options are available in a wide range of styles and materials.

If possible, devote an entire wall, from floor to ceiling, for built-in storage to make the final effect more seamless and to blend in with the room. You can also fit out alcoves or recesses to good effect. Fitted wardrobes can even be designed to fit round awkward angles, sloping ceilings and uneven walls, making the most of the space. However, they are usually more expensive than freestanding wardrobes and often need to be fitted by an expert.

WALK-IN WARDROBES

Mostly we consider walk-in wardrobes as a luxury, but they can represent a good use of space. If you are fortunate enough to have a large bedroom, consider partitioning off a section of the room and creating a walk-in wardrobe with open shelves and rails. Alternatively, in a smaller bedroom you may be able to adapt this idea by taking some space, perhaps from an adjacent corridor, landing or spare room. This would mean knocking through a bedroom wall and dividing off a small area. While this may seem like a lot of work, it would ensure that your bedroom is a calm and clutter-free retreat.

Mirrored panels on the front of this wardrobe (see right) are useful and also reflect colours around the room.

Fit a large wardrobe into a recess to make the best use of space. The panelled effect helps the doors blend into the rest of the room.

OTHER BEDROOM FURNITURE

Creating the right atmosphere for sleep and relaxation is the
objective of good bedroom design, along with essential
storage and attention to detail.

As well as wardrobes, you also need to think about other
storage needs for your bedroom or bedroom/study.
Ideally, it is a good idea to include bedside cabinets, a
chest of drawers and/or a dressing table/desk. In reality,
most of us have to compromise between essential
furniture, a comfortable space and the practicalities of
moving around the room.

If you have limited space for a chest of drawers or
dressing table, you could explore the possibility of fitting
a compact set of drawers into an existing wardrobe, with
a pull-out section to use as a dressing table. For an extra
surface in the bedroom, think about adding a shelf above

a picture rail. Use it to store paperbacks or all those bits
and bobs that can create clutter on bedside cabinets
– it can also provide a neat solution for displaying
decorative objects.

Another good use of space is to go for a small chest
of drawers either side of a double bed, rather than a
bedside cabinet. Many companies produce slimline

units, with five or six drawers, that function as bedside tables. However, if you can fit a chest of drawers or dressing table into your bedroom, it will certainly prove very useful and can double up as a desk.

DRESSING TABLES

Once considered an essential piece of bedroom furniture, dressing tables aren't for everyone, but the latest dressing tables are compact, chic and provide a stylish space for lotions and potions. If you fancy a styling zone in your bedroom, with everything to hand, then opt for a dressing table. Make-up and jewellery can be hidden away in the drawers or on top in lovely boxes or baskets. Some have mirrors built in, or you could add a freestanding vanity mirror that suits your style. Options include: an Art Deco console table in birch and mirrored glass, a painted dressing table with a feminine feel, a leather and chrome table which can double up as a desk, a unisex dark oak design and a modern classic in oak with a matching stool. You could even buy a handmade trunk, with a hardened canvas exterior; these have masses of storage – mini drawers, compartments, etc. – making them ideal for a bedroom that's tight on space.

Of course, you could opt for an antique or vintage dressing table; they come in many shapes and sizes, and not only provide a practical place to put on the glamour, but also make a big style impact in a bedroom.

MIRRORS

Bedrooms definitely need at least one mirror, whether it sits on the dressing table or chest of drawers, on a wall, or is full length. Make a style statement with a distinctive mirror, which will make a room look brighter and bigger. A full-length mirror is extremely useful for getting ready.

With so many shapes and sizes, mirrors are a versatile decorative element that gives instant elegance to a bedroom with very little effort. They can brighten up dark corners and there's a mirror for everyone's taste.

In a bedroom, shelving can be used for many different functions.

With antique furniture, consider reupholstering to add pattern and texture.

Here, the imposing stone fireplace that could dominate the room has been given a quirky touch with a display of soup tins.

Interest has been added to the large wall facing the bed with a painted white section; the useful shelf that marks the end of the vertical could double as a dressing table or work area.

This luxurious sleigh bed has been made
even more sumptuous with the addition of
a canopy suspended from the ceiling.

In this room a window seat, with pretty Roman blinds above, provides a serene place to sit.

The painted floor adds to the feeling of space in this rustic, softly coloured bedroom that has been decorated with quirky, vintage-style pieces.

The feature wall behind this elaborate wooden bed has been set inside a 'frame' made from Edwardian-style architrave.

This serene scheme of muted greys includes a subtle, wallpaper-like pattern that has been stencilled onto one wall.

CHILDREN'S ROOMS

From a calm and comforting nursery for a newborn baby
to a teenager's cool, high-tech hang-out, a child's room
needs to change as much as they do.

BABIES

Nurseries for young babies should
be calm and comforting spaces,
both to allow them to sleep as easily
and soundly as possible, and also to
provide a peaceful place for feeding
and changing.

Moses baskets, cribs or small cots
are ideal for the first few months
when parents want to keep the
baby in their bedroom. Tiny babies
will be happy in fairly enclosed
spaces; however, they are not
absolutely essential, as they will be
quickly outgrown. Cots that allow
you to adjust the height of the
mattress as the baby grows provide
more flexibility. When a small crib
or basket has been outgrown – at
about 3–6 months – it is a good
idea to move the baby into a proper
cot in his or her own room to
encourage a settled sleep routine.
You can buy two-in-one cot beds
that will turn into grown-up beds
when the baby gets older.

NURSERY FURNITURE

Choose well-made furniture for
strength, safety, flexibility and good
looks. For babies and very young
children, storage should be adult-
orientated for ease of changing,
feeding and dressing. A chest of
drawers is more useful than a
wardrobe as a baby's clothes tend
to be folded rather than hung up;

in addition, a changing mat can be added on the top.

A shelf close to the changing mat is very useful for storing all the necessary creams, etc., within easy reach. Shelving makes good all-purpose storage for toys, games and picture books (and for books, computer games and DVDs later); position shelves so the baby can see and enjoy them from the cot.

This is a room where you will spend a great deal of time, so add a comfortable low chair for nursing the baby.

Like beds, under cot spaces make good storage areas; you can buy storage boxes on castors, which makes access even easier.

CURTAINS AND BLINDS

Windows in a nursery will need either curtains or blinds to block out all light when the baby needs to sleep. These can be any colour, as long as curtains are lined with blackout material and blinds are blackout quality. Alternatively, you could combine some pretty unlined voile curtains with a blackout blind. Opt for delicate shades and tactile fabrics for extra cosiness. Consider keeping walls neutral and choosing simple wall stickers to add interest.

Lighting should be bright so that you can see what you're doing when changing and dressing babies, but soft for night feeds. A dimmer switch is ideal in a baby's room.

Stickers and feature walls are easy ways to liven up a baby's room.

Dos and don'ts

▶ Don't position the cot or bed underneath a window, directly against a radiator or with shelves or appliances above that a child can get hold of.

▶ Avoid hanging heavy pictures or mirrors above the cot or bed.

▶ Secure all tall or heavy items of furniture by fixing it to the wall with anti-toppling devices such as fixing brackets.

▶ Use socket covers to keep plug sockets safe from probing fingers.

▶ Keep trailing lamp cords out of children's reach, to prevent injury from pulling on them.

▶ Fit window locks and latches so that windows will only open up to 10cm (4in).

▶ Bunk beds are not suitable for children under six years old.

YOUNG CHILDREN

A child's room can give you a great deal of scope for design;
it can look as smart and stylish as any other room in the house.

When choosing paint colour or wallpaper, it's a good idea to allow children a say in the decoration – if he or she is involved the chances are that the room will be treated with greater care and consideration. Walls need to be finished in a surface that is tough and easy to clean, such as washable paint or wallpaper. Children grow out of fads quickly, so rather than decorate a complete room in the latest cartoon-hero wallpaper or converting it into an authentic pirate ship, use a neutral background and introduce colour with bed linen, curtains or blinds, or maybe with stickers and fun accessories. A feature wall is also a good way of turning a nursery into a bedroom.

BEDS AND FURNITURE

When it's time for your child to move out of their cot, choose between a toddler bed and a full-sized bed. Toddler beds come in a wide range of styles and colours, and some are extendable to keep up with your growing child. However, a full-size bed, fitted with safety rails, is a better long-term buy than a child's bed.

Stringent safety regulations govern the dimensions of bunk beds, and they are not advisable for children under six years old. However, they are space-saving, providing two beds in a room that would not

accommodate two beds side by side, or where they would be very cramped; and, of course, children love climbing up to bed. Cabin beds are also a good option, because there is lots of fitted storage underneath. Some children's beds are versatile and can be turned upside down, allowing you to have a low bed or a high bed. The space underneath is perfect for extending the floor space/play area, storage or an extra mattress for sleepovers.

Upcycling is not just for adults; give your child's room a unique personality with upcycled furniture – a chest of drawers or wardrobe. You could even use a combination of paint and wallpaper, for instance, and paint the frame of the drawers or wardrobe and jazz up the drawer fronts or doors with wallpaper offcuts.

Use all of the space in the bedroom. If an alcove or recess is not being utilised, try adding some shelves (see page 101), and you can then use them to display books or an assortment of items.

PLAYING

Energetic toddlers need a play area as well as a secure and cosy bed to snuggle down in at night.

Children also love to draw, and you can create a semi-permanent drawing space if you paint a panel or a section of a wardrobe door with blackboard paint – with a few sticks of chalk, they will always have somewhere to express themselves. Keep the rest of the door white or a pale colour so that the black doesn't dominate the space.

Children often have to share a room. If possible, provide each with a clearly defined area. It doesn't have to be divided equally; ages and interests will be a determining factor. If it's not possible to divide the space, provide some kind of base or private place where they can keep their special possessions or hide them away.

TEENAGERS

Create a versatile bed/sitting room for your teenager, that incorporates space
to sleep, study and entertain, together with clever storage.

Teenagers can be pretty tough customers when it comes to designing a bedroom, they will have their own ideas, so include them when deciding on a scheme. Most teenagers want a more adult room – a living-room-cum-study-cum-bedroom. Let them experiment with colours and designs that you might not choose for yourself. If they choose the main colour you can then help them to pick a scheme that works well around it.

BEDS
One of the main concerns in a teenager's room is to make the bed look more like a sofa. Divans are ideal because they can be pushed against a wall in a corner with plenty of cushions and used as seating, as well as for sleeping. In addition, they often provide storage space underneath.

A loft bed or sleeping platform is a good idea, especially if you have limited space, although the ceiling must be reasonably high. Raising the level of the bed leaves space underneath for a study, relaxing or storage area. If you use the space for a study then it will also free up wall space for notice boards, posters or photographs.

If there's room for a small sofabed as well as a bed, there'll be plenty of seating when friends are round – and it will convert into a bed if someone needs to sleep over.

STORAGE

Not necessarily, but almost inevitably, teenagers are messy and unconcerned about being tidy. All you can do is just provide as much storage as you can and encourage them to use it. Respect his or her privacy and so don't go in unasked and tidy up yourself.

Furniture need not be brand new; vintage finds mixed with new pieces can create a quirky look for a teenager, and they might like to customise old furniture themselves.

Clothing is important to teenagers so make sure there is plenty of cupboard and drawer space: a built-in or freestanding wardrobe and a large chest of drawers with dividers to keep things organised.

STUDYING

An organised study area is important for teenagers; they need a desk or table to do homework and to study for exams, as well as for hobbies. Allow space for a computer, and shelving for other papers, pens and pencils and books.

Tips for teenagers' rooms

▸ **Laundry basket:** Buy a large one, it's a simple way to stop clothes piling up on the floor.
▸ **Edit belongings:** Get rid of clothes and any outgrown games, books, etc. so as not to clog up storage. Do it together with your teenage son or daughter, never behind their back.
▸ **Instant update:** Change bed linen, lampshades and rugs if your teenager tires of a scheme, or you want a quick makeover. And colourful, removable stickers are great for updating plain walls.
▸ **Floor cushions and beanbags:** These provide relaxed seating for chill-out areas.
▸ **A full-length mirror:** Most teenagers like to check out how they look.
▸ **Lighting:** Flexibility is key; dimmers provide mood changes but make sure there is good light for reading by the desk and at the bedside.

In this grown-up
girl's room, pale pink
paint contrasts with a
dramatic feature wall
and matching curtains.

Adjustable lighting provides both general and specific illumination either for reading in bed or sitting down; the fittings used here are ingenious as well as pretty.

Quirky touches can make childrens' rooms more fun: here, a sloping picture rail can be used as a marble or toy car run.

Every Lego-lover's dream: Perspex cubes provide a great way to display creations, while the bricks have been sorted by colour and stored in a handyman's organiser.

BATHROOMS

Combine the practical and the indulgent to create a bathroom haven that's
as luxurious as it is good-looking.

When planning a bathroom, ask yourself who will use it and how often, as well as how much space is available. Have you got room for a bath and a walk-in shower? Do you want a bidet, a pair of basins (handy if there are two of you getting ready for work at the same time), a built-in linen cupboard or a heated towel rail? Will space-saving fittings make a difference? It is always a good idea to plan everything carefully on graph paper, noting the positions of pipes, windows and doors, and allowing generous activity space for knees, elbows, drying and so on around each fitting. If possible, it is visually neater to run pipes under floors and behind slim false walls. And it's not wasted space – punch shallow shelves and cupboards into the false walls and you can create fabulously useful fitted storage.

KEEP IT SIMPLE

Bathroom fittings are available in a multitude of styles and prices, but simplicity is often the best way forward: plain, inexpensive designs can look wonderful when teamed with interesting accessories, and a sensible option is to invest more in moving parts, such as shower doors and taps. How a bathroom feels is vital, in terms of textures and temperatures against bare skin, and underfloor heating gives an efficient, overall heat, while freeing up space against the walls – perhaps for a statement towel warmer. And lighting is important in creating an efficient atmosphere for a quick morning shower, or a more relaxing ambience for an evening bath.

Careful planning will ensure that your new bathroom meets all your needs.

Iridescent mosaic tiles add sparkle to this wet-room design.

Quick ways to revamp your tiles

1 If you don't like the colour or pattern of your tiles, paint over them. First, sand the tiles to scuff the surface and then clean both the tiles and the grout scrupulously with sugar soap. Apply tile paint with either a natural bristle brush or a gloss roller. If the colour change is dramatic, you may need a second coat. Leave to dry, then redraw the grout lines with a special pen.

2 Give plain tiles a makeover with stickers – they come in a number of different designs, and are durable, wipeable and, if you change your mind, you can just take them off. They are relatively easy to apply (the surface must be smooth and clean), provided you mark their positions carefully.

3 To rejuvenate discoloured grout, either use a grout pen or, if your grout is beyond repair, remove it with a grout rake, clean up and apply fresh grout. It will look as good as new. You can also freshen up old sealant by scraping it out carefully with a knife blade and reapplying using a mould-resistant type.

PRACTICAL ISSUES

A new bathroom is an asset to any home, but before you replace your
old one or refurbish an existing one, it's important to know about basic
plumbing and the relevant building regulations.

Once bathroom fittings are plumbed in they are permanent fixtures that you are unlikely to want to change, so planning is essential. Sometimes planning a small bathroom can be easy: given you have to house a minimum of three units – bath or shower, basin and WC – and take account of windows and doors, there may only be one solution in terms of layout. In addition, you must consider the plumbing and drainage. For instance, unless you want to go to great expense of rerouting pipes, the WC has to be sited close to the existing soil stack, so this gives you a starting point.

Plumbing can be costly, so it is worth aiming for a streamlined solution for bathrooms. Bringing water to the bathroom and downstairs loo is more efficient the nearer they are to the source of supply. Unless you have a combination boiler, cold water has to come from the tank (often in the roof space), but hot water comes from the cylinder – bathrooms and cylinders should ideally be placed close to one another, so that the pipe that runs to the boiler or other source of hot water is not too long. A combination boiler heats the water directly from the mains, so there is no need to have a water tank or hot-water cylinder.

If you choose a roll-top bath, make sure your floor is able to take the weight when it is full of water.

Cupboards built under sinks can help conceal pipework as well as providing storage.

High-level cisterns provide a good flush, but you have to have enough ceiling height to install one.

Most houses have their waste, i.e. waste from kitchens and bathrooms, run into one main drain, so it is more economical in terms of plumbing to site the kitchen and bathroom on the same side of the house.

BUILDING REGULATIONS

When you are refitting a bathroom with new units, you do not generally need building regulations approval, except possibly for drainage and electricals. However, for new bathrooms in extensions, or where there hasn't been one before, building regulations approval is likely to be required to ensure that the room will have adequate ventilation and drainage (and meet requirements in respect of structural stability, electrical and fire safety). Check with your local authority.

VENTILATION

In bathrooms, ventilation is vital; moisture in the air can lead to condensation and mould growth, which could spread to the rest of the house. So building regulations are quite strict in this respect. If you wish to know more about the building regulations and ventilation you can download them for free at www.planningportal.gov.uk/ approved documents.

BATHROOM BASICS

Bear in mind that in bathrooms surface decoration needs to be tough, waterproof and easy to clean, so it can withstand wear and tear from extremes of temperature, steam and moisture.

FLOORS

First and foremost, bathroom floors need to be water-resistant and easy to clean – a hard surface is preferable. There is a wide range of choices: sheet vinyl or tiles, stone, slate, porcelain or ceramic tiles and laminate flooring (suitable for bathrooms). Wooden flooring can be used in a bathroom as long as it has an appropriate durable finish.

If a new bathroom is installed in a room where the floor is constructed of timber joists and boards, there is a risk of the floor being overloaded from the bath once it is full of water – therefore, the floor may need to be strengthened. A structural engineer will be able to assess the floor and determine this for you.

WALLS

Paint is the easiest and most inexpensive way of decorating bathroom walls, provided they are in good

Decorating tips

▶ Using colour in a bathroom can provide a welcome accent of vitality and interest – a single colour is enough.

▶ Mirrors are an invaluable way of enhancing space in the bathroom.

▶ Pay attention to detailing; junctions between different finishes should be as neat and inconspicuous as possible.

▶ Reflective surfaces, such as stainless steel and glass mosaic tiles, bounce the light around.

▶ Don't limit yourself to bathroom-specific shelves and cabinets; consider stainless steel racks from kitchen suppliers or other open-shelf systems.

condition. Use a washable paint or wallpaper, or non-washable wallpaper protected with a clear varnish.

Ceramic tiles, glass mosaic tiles, tongue-and-groove panelling (see page 60) and the latest wet-wall panels/PVC cladding are all options. Wet-wall panels and PVC bathroom cladding come in a wide range of designs, from classic stone and marble effects, to modern designs with a sparkling or iridescent finish.

LIGHTING

Direct lighting is essential for applying make-up, grooming and shaving. This could be combined with more indirect light for bathing.

Downlights recessed in the ceiling are neater and safer than pendant lights. Wall lights, either side of a mirror should be aimed at the face. Alternatively, you could always add a mirror with film star-style bulbs around the frame.

Sometimes mirrored bathroom cabinets have built-in lighting, which can be useful.

STORAGE

Restrict visual clutter to essential items only, such as towels, soap and toothbrushes. Try to build in storage wherever possible, underneath basins and between the basin and WC, or at either end of the bath. A cupboard under a basin can conceal pipe work and provide storage at the same time.

A simple solution for the basics – soap, nailbrush and facecloth – is a rack across the bath. These are particularly useful if you have a roll-top bathtub. Gels and lotions also need to be stored in shower enclosures: if possible, incorporate a recess shelf in the wall at the design stage. Otherwise there is a wide range of racks available. In addition, a shelf near to the basin is important for basic toiletries.

Bathroom cabinets are useful for storing medicines and toiletries. Store medicines out of the reach of children; either use a medicine cabinet with a child-proof catch or secure a conventional cupboard.

You will need plenty of space for towels; rails should be within easy reach of the bath or shower.

FIXTURES AND FITTINGS

Bathroom fittings determine the look of the whole room.
There is a wealth of different types to choose from, but
make sure they also suit your needs and your budget.

When choosing baths, showers, basins and loos, cast your inhibitions aside. In the showroom, stand in the shower, climb into the bath and sit on the loo. It's the only way to tell whether they are comfortable and feel well-made. And ask your retailer how products have been tested, whether they conform to British or European standards and what guarantee is on offer.

Baths: The more you pay for a bath, the more variety there is in size, shape and material. A standard bath is a 1,700 x 700mm (67 x 27½in) rectangle, but you can also find double-ended and freestanding baths, and a variety of shapes. Acrylic is most common but, if money were no object, you could choose a bath made from stone, wood, copper or glass.

Showers: Look for three key features: flow control,

thermostatic control and easy cleaning. The more you pay, the more features you get, including accurate constant temperature control, a hot-water safety limiter, cool housing, water-saving, adjustable sprays and easy-clean functions.

Basins: The traditional option is a pedestal style in ceramic, but there are lots of other styles, including winged, semi-pedestal, counter-top or wall-hung. You can tell a good-quality basin by its weight and clean, straight lines.

WCs: Basic loos are of the pan and cistern variety, but if you pay a little more you could go for a close-coupled style (the pan and cistern are in one seamless unit), a back-to-wall WC where the cistern is hidden behind either a false wall or furniture, or a swish, wall-hung type.

WET ROOMS

If you enjoy an indulgent shower then a wet room is an interesting option – it's simply a waterproof, walk-in shower area (pretty much any shape or size you like), with a drain in the floor, a drenching showerhead and (sometimes) a glass screen. Spacious and stylish, wet rooms are often seen as the last word in luxury, but there are pitfalls. Wet room walls and floors must be made completely watertight by covering with sheeting or sealant. You will also need a suitable drainage slope (or a pre-formed tray), high water pressure and – to prevent condensation and mould – tip top ventilation.

TIME TO RELAX

▶ **Hydro-massage baths:** Designed to reduce stress, relax and rejuvenate, hydro-massage baths bubble away your aches and pains just like a masseur's fingers. They can also improve circulation and skin tone, and help you sleep. There are two distinct types of operation: whirlpool baths, which usually have half a dozen or so strong jets of water directed at specific areas, and spa baths, featuring hundreds of tiny holes in the base of the bath which bubble air upwards for a softer, fizzy feeling over the whole body.

▶ **Chromatherapy:** For the last word in relaxation, try chromatherapy in the bath or shower. A sequence of coloured lights washes through the water or steam, and can be paused, if you wish, to complement your mood. It's said that reds, oranges and yellows boost circulation and stimulate the senses, while blues, greens and pinks relax the mind and body.

▶ **Aromatherapy:** Some baths and showers offer built-in aromatherapy, where essential oils are diffused as a gentle, scented mist to aid physiological and mental wellbeing. Lavender, for example, is a staple for relaxation and sleep-inducement, while grapefruit boosts energy and eucalyptus clears the mind.

▶ **Super showers:** Shower poles (or towers) combine

several body sprays, ranging from a fine mist to a powerful drench, the former sometimes mixing air with water for a rain-like effect, the latter perhaps coming from a 'blade' showerhead. If you want to get gadgety, digital programming means that you can control the various elements of your shower from a single interface, with pre-programmed massage and temperature therapies for a truly spa-like experience. For an even more multi-functional shower, just add steam. Basic requirements are vapour-tight doors, a steam generator and a seat, but to that can be added foot massage, hands-free telephone, MP3 connection and waterproof TV.

Wall-hung sinks and a contemporary freestanding bath.

Whirlpool baths give you a spa-like experience in your own home.

CHOOSING BATHROOM FITTINGS

Usually, a bathroom will include a bath, shower, basin and loo, but your final
choice will depend on the type and size of your bathroom – family, secondary or
en suite – personal choice and, of course, how much you want to spend.

Research the market thoroughly so that you are aware of the full range of bathroom fittings available. In a showroom you can stand at a basin, sit on a toilet and even lie in a bathtub, to help you assess whether such fixtures suit you.

BATHS

▸ In a small room you may not have any choice but to position the bath along one wall; however, many manufacturers produce compact fixtures for small bathrooms.

▸ There is no real need to match sanitaryware; many styles of basin go with a Victorian-style roll-top bath, but be aware of non-matching fittings, they may be all white but shades can vary considerably.

▸ Sleek, modern sanitaryware can look good in a feature-filled period home. Equally, traditional-style fittings can look fantastic in modern homes.

▸ For a freestanding bath on a budget, make a frame around it and clad a simple bath in tiles, mirror or stone.

▸ Corner and offset baths can offer a good use of space.

▸ Designer baths are expensive, but when you want to make an impact in your bathroom, consider a freestanding egg-shaped bath, a wooden or glass tub. Generally, this type of bath takes up a lot of space.

▸ Roll-tops are also statement bathtubs; they've developed from the standard Victorian cast-iron variety to imposing, luxury copper and zinc bathtubs. Usually, as with designer baths, roll-tops do not work in small spaces, and they are somewhat impractical as there is nowhere handy to put soap and other bath products. Be aware that some reproduction acrylic roll-tops are not well made and can look cheap and tacky.

SHOWERS

▸ Showers are more economical and space-saving than baths. Most people find that they are more convenient, and some question the need for a bath, especially as there are so many fantastic designs for showers available.

▸ Ideally, for the best of both worlds, install a separate shower unit in the bathroom, but if you don't have room, fit a good-quality shower over the bath, along with a glass door.

▸ Shower enclosure (cubicle) designs have become simpler and less cluttered; there are now walk-in options, curved glass panels and low-level trays.

▸ A custom-built, tiled alcove is a good-looking alternative to a ready-made unit.

▸ Fixed overhead showers can look fantastic, but, remember, getting your hair wet is unavoidable.

▸ Wet rooms, where the shower is not contained, maximise available floor space (see page 197).

▸ If you have plenty of space, walk-in showers with a 'dry' area at one end where you can hang towels are another option.

▶ Most importantly, make sure that there is sufficient pressure to deliver a shower worth having.

BASINS AND WCS

▶ Basins come in all shapes and sizes – round, oval, square and rectangular. Similarly, WCs are no longer standard, and are available in a wide range of designs.

▶ Corner basins and WCs are available and can help make the most of space.

▶ Wall-hung basins and loos keep the floor clear and make a bathroom feel bigger, but you will need to make sure that the wall can take the weight.

▶ Only go for a glass basin if you are happy with the amount of cleaning involved.

▶ Choose a basin that is as large as space permits, deep enough to bend over easily when washing your face, and wide enough to accommodate wet elbows.

Sink units with drawers underneath are another good storage solution.

Mirror-fronted bathroom cabinets combine two useful functions in one.

FINISHING TOUCHES

With some thoughtful finishing touches and a few gorgeous accessories, even
the most basic of bathrooms can be transformed into a stylish sanctuary.

TIP-TOP TAPS

Change the taps (a quick and easy
job for any plumber) and an old
basin will take on a whole new
look. In the same vein, it's also easy
enough to replace the handset on
many showers.

SITTING PRETTY

Put a new seat on your loo. A
simple white style will freshen up
the overall look, while a wooden
one has a natural, homely effect. Or
you could opt for a funky, modern
seat featuring bold colours and
patterns – anything from a Union
Jack to fish, glitter or barbed wire.

SHOWER POWER

Swap a mouldy old shower curtain
for a fresh new one – or even replace
it with a glamorous glass screen.

TILE STYLE

Changing small areas of tiling need
not be too arduous – eye-catching
mosaic is ideal, or else a sleek glass
panel in a dramatic colour.

MIRROR, MIRROR

A new mirror is great for increasing
the sense of light and space, and
vital for all sorts of bathroom
activities. It can also become a
decorative feature in its own right.

TREAT YOUR WINDOWS

A new window treatment makes a world of difference. Blinds are cost-effective and can be co-ordinated with your overall scheme, while window film is fun, inexpensive and easy to apply.

SORT YOUR STORAGE

Co-ordinate all your small storage items, from wicker baskets to crackle-glazed pots or bright plastic tubs; it's all about setting the scene with colour, pattern and texture.

ART ON THE WALL

Add beautifully framed paintings or photographs (though perhaps not in very humid areas) to add character and interest.

HOTEL-STYLE LUXURY

Buy a new set of co-ordinating towels – the larger and fluffier the better. It's an inexpensive change that will make you feel like a star.

A bathroom on a budget

- ▶ No-frills white bathroom fittings are much cheaper than designer ones – use tiles, taps and accessories to create an elegant and upmarket effect. But remember that not all whites are quite the same shade. It can be tricky to match them if you are buying from a variety of online retailers.
- ▶ Plan your new bathroom carefully so as to avoid moving existing plumbing – and keep installation costs down.
- ▶ A radiator that doubles up as a towel rail will save you buying the two items separately.
- ▶ Save on tiling by only going up to half-height around the room, or else just tile the splashbacks next to the bath and basin. Use paint elsewhere.

Feature walls aren't just for bedrooms and living rooms – try one in your bathroom, too, with some stunning, colourful tiles.

Wall displays can also be highly effective in a bathroom – they provide a focal point and can complement your design scheme.

These wall-hung sinks exhibit all the features of a high-end basin: clean, straight lines, a good weight and a quality finish.

Roll-top baths are statement pieces, but remember that they are unlikely to work in small spaces.

DETAILS THAT COUNT

What's the difference between four walls and a roof, and a place
that is welcoming, nurturing and an all-round great place to be?
Well, the former is a house and the latter is a home.

A house may look really smart, but a home is where you kick off your shoes, cook up a storm, cuddle the kids, make a mess, laugh, cry and generally live your life. So, while there are plenty of decorating guidelines to help you put together a picture-perfect house, remember that, in creating a home, you should do what suits you best. If you can create a comfortable space for family and friends who fill the house with fun and laughter, you have that wonderful thing: a happy home.

In a truly comfortable home, every room is as relaxing and welcoming as it is stylish. It looks right but, just as importantly, it feels right in every way. It could be big or small, period or modern, filled with antique treasures or high-street buys; it could be a single person's pad or a bustling family house – the key is that you love it, and that you love being in it. In winter, a comfortable home is warm and cosy; in summer, it is light, bright and airy. And the secret to all this? It's decorating with your senses: sight, touch and, yes, even smell and sound. Colours, patterns, shapes, styles and textures appeal to these first two senses, while the materials you choose (especially for flooring and worktops) will determine whether your home is filled with noises that are loud or soft, tinny or tinkling, high or low.

*The art and accessories
you choose echo your
personal sense of style.*

Smells can be generated by creative cooking in a fabulous kitchen, deliciously scented candles or gently fragranced laundry, or something more sinister such as blocked drains or a mouldy cupboard. The way in which you design your home can influence all of these things for good or bad. It may not be obvious, but it is important. With this in mind, your decorative efforts will come together as a gorgeous, holistic whole – and all year round you will have a blissful home that has heart and soul, is calm and energising, refreshes your senses and is a joy to live in.

Small touches can make a big difference: the lavender in the back of this chair not only looks attractive, it fragrances the room, too.

Fun and informal, colourful beanbags are ideal for a family home.

DOOR AND WINDOW FURNITURE
AND LIGHT SWITCHES

When choosing ironmongery and other finishing touches that
will be on show, think about which type suits your home;
these details all contribute to the overall look.

Details count not only in terms of style but also practicality – convenience, ease of use, smooth working over time and with low maintenance. Decent handles, doorknobs, window fittings and light switches can be surprisingly costly; it's worth investing in good-quality designs as it will make a difference. Apart from the huge DIY stores, there are some amazing specialist shops. It is worth visiting some to help you decide exactly what you want before the builder or electrician turns up with their own supply of fittings.

An element of consistency is important, particularly in a small space. Ideally, stick to the same type of detail in the same material in every area of your home. For example, if you have brushed metal door handles in the living areas, you should have the same in the bedroom.

DOOR FURNITURE

With such a wealth of products available it's not always easy to decide on the right hardware for your front door and internal doors. Take your lead from the age, style and character of your home. Broadly speaking, there are three main categories: contemporary, classic and

Antique hardware, and sometimes even matching sets, can be found in antique, architectural-salvage companies or second-hand shops. Otherwise there is vast range of excellent reproduction hardware to choose from.

WINDOW FURNITURE

Appropriate hardware is important for the security and smooth operation of windows. As with door furniture, the type you choose will depend on the style of your house. Brass, chrome, nickel and antique black are just some of the finishes available. Aim for consistency throughout the home, although you could differentiate between downstairs and upstairs.

LIGHT SWITCHES AND SOCKETS

Electrical fittings are another range of details that count. They have to meet British Standards – a minimum quality for the materials used as well as a minimum requirement for performance and insulation. Make sure all your fittings conform to these standards and then choose the style. There are lots of finishes to choose from, including standard white plastic, brass, brushed steel, chrome, wood and antique copper. You can buy clear Perspex switches and switches that match the colour of your room. However, light switches do not have to be a feature, the most important thing is that they should blend into the wall.

traditional. If you live in a modern house or flat then it makes sense to go for a contemporary style, such as stainless steel handles on internal doors. A country house looks best with simple wrought-iron fittings on both the front door and internal doors. For a period-style home, choose more elaborate traditional or classic fittings. On a Victorian panelled door you could go for classic, plain white china doorknobs.

SOFT FURNISHINGS

From the softest cashmere to the hardest-wearing denim, you can create your
own, individual look and style with irresistible soft furnishings.

Patterned, textured or plain, subtle or spectacular,
fabrics can transform a room. But picking the right fabric
for covering a sofa or making a blind can be a tricky
business. While budget, personal taste and the overall
decoration of the room are key factors, they're not the
only considerations. From a practical point of view, it is
important to match the fabric to the intended project. So,
before you start, make sure you know your silks from your
synthetics and your cottons from your corduroys.

HOW TO CHOOSE FABRIC

▶ Always ask for a swatch or, even better, borrow or buy a
  length of fabric so you can see how it will look in situ.
▶ Wider fabric is often better value. Less sewing may be
  required, too.
▶ Heavier fabrics are usually too bulky for small projects;
  lighter fabrics tend to wear more quickly.
▶ Check how the fabric is categorised: for light, general
  or heavy domestic use. And look for 'rub test' figures –
  16,000 or above is suitable for general domestic use.
▶ Is it washable, and at what temperature?
  Will it shrink?
▶ Large patterns require more fabric so that you can
  match the repeats, and can end up being much more
  expensive than plains or small patterns.

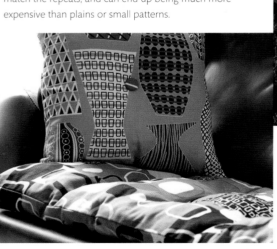

HOW ARE FABRICS MADE?

Fabrics are composed of natural or synthetic fibres,
or blends of them. They can be plain or woven with
a pattern. Printing is done by machine or by hand,
or digitally using computer technology (which allows
small, personalised runs). Most fabrics are available in a
variety of weights.

A quick guide to weaves

Bouclé has a looped pile.

Corduroy features pile in stripes.

Damasks contrast matt and shiny areas of pattern; usually rather traditional.

Jacquards feature a complex, raised pattern.

Moiré has a watermark pattern; often on silks.

Satin is heavy with a lustrous surface, usually in silk or polyester.

Twill weave produces diagonal or zigzag lines on the surface.

Velvet may be made from a variety of fibres, and features a luxurious, soft pile.

FIBRES

▶ **Cotton:** Ranging from lightweight muslin to heavy canvas, cotton dyes and prints well, and is easy to care for.

▶ **Linen:** It has a lovely drape and lustre, but linen creases easily (so is often mixed with other fibres).

▶ **Nylon, or polyamide:** Man-made fibres are tough and resist abrasion, but tend to produce static electricity.

▶ **Polyester:** This is a very strong synthetic fibre that mixes well with other fibres. It can be washed frequently and on high temperatures.

▶ **Silk:** It comes in intense colours and has an attractive, lustrous surface, but silk is delicate.

▶ **Viscose:** Made from wood pulp, viscose is hardwearing and durable.

▶ **Wool:** Breathable, warm and naturally water-resistant, wool varies from heavy sheep's wool to fine cashmere. It will shrink and felt if washed and spun at too high a temperature.

▶ **Oilcloth:** This is cotton that has been coated with a PVC resin or acrylic to make it waterproof. Although durable and wipeable, it can stain and isn't heat-resistant.

UPHOLSTERY

Choose fabrics wisely and you will get the best from them.
For covering sofas and chairs, there's an endless choice of colours,
patterns and textures, but practicality is important, too.

Hardwearing, tightly woven fabrics are the best choice for most upholstered furniture, though in some cases (a seldom-used bedroom chair, for example) a more decorative fabric, such as silk, is fine. Medium- to heavy-weight cottons and cotton mixes, linen mixes and wools are all good choices, while corduroy, denim and low-pile velvet have appealing textures and should be long-lasting. Avoid deep piles, which may become crushed, and loose or loopy weaves, which are likely to catch and snag.

Upholstering with plains is pretty straightforward, but make sure that any nap runs in the same direction when all the pieces are made up. Stripes should run straight and be aligned and, if you choose a bold pattern, you will need to centre the motifs on sofa or chair backs, seats and cushions (this can mean buying a lot of fabric). For new and replacement upholstery and loose covers, whatever fabric you choose should usually be fire-retardant, though it is sometimes possible to use a non-fire-retardant fabric over a fire-retardant interlining – always check with the manufacturer or retailer.

Fresh upholstery makes a radical difference to old furniture.

It is relatively easy to make a new cover for a beanbag, or to re-cover a seat, box lid or stool.

LOOSE COVERS

A great way to give a new lease of life to any fabric-covered furniture, from a sofa to a dining chair, loose covers can also be used to alter a piece's proportions and even its overall character. Style-wise, they can be sleek and chic, casually unstructured or frilly and flouncy – depending on how they are cut and whether they are designed with a zip or ties, pleats or gathers, piping or a valance. Pick a fabric that is washable, and substantial enough to hold its shape yet soft enough to be comfortable; medium-weight cottons, linens or blends, or light wools, are all ideal.

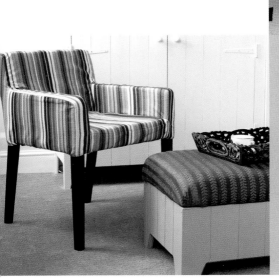

Re-covering seats, boxes and beanbags

Take the seat out of the chair frame and carefully remove the old covering. Lay the seat onto your fabric, positioning it carefully so that any pattern is centred or aligned. Draw about 10cm (4in) around the seat and cut the fabric out, then use a staple gun to attach it – quite taut but not overly stretched – first at the centre of each side, then at the corners, and then in-between. Make sure the fabric is even and the corners are neat. Drop the seat back into the frame and re-attach. To re-cover the padded lid of a box, remove its hinges and treat as a chair seat. Screw the hinges back on and re-attach. Give a bean bag a new lease of life with a replacement cover. Remove the old cover (leaving the filling in the liner) and take it apart, then use it as a template to cut out your new fabric. Stitch together securely, adding a zip, hook-and-loop tape or other form of fastening.

ACCESSORIES

*Both practical and beautiful, accessories create a unique sense
of personal style. Use them in every room of your home.*

CUSHIONS

A new cushion will instantly brighten up a boring sofa or
chair and add visual interest to a room – use the colour
and pattern either to pull a scheme together or create
a dynamic contrast. It's easy to make your own cushion
cover – or, if sewing's not your thing, inexpensive to have
them made for you. You can use almost any fabric, within
reason and, as you will only need a small amount, you can
go for something quite luxurious – a square metre should
make four average-sized cushion fronts, then you can
use cheaper fabric for the back. Alternatively, try pieces
of vintage fabric for an eclectic look, and have fun with
different shapes, sizes, trims and fastenings.

TABLE LINEN

For tablecloths, runners and napkins, light- to medium-
weight cottons, linens and cotton or linen blends are
best. Damasks are a traditional choice, and a hand-
embroidered tablecloth can look very pretty. But above all,
if you are going to use them every day, choose fabrics that
will withstand frequent washing, reserving the delicates for
special occasions. For the last word in ease of cleaning,
your best bet is oilcloth, a plastic-coated cloth that simply
wipes down with a damp cloth and comes in a massive
range of gorgeous colours and patterns.

THROWS AND BEDSPREADS

If you want to transform a bedroom in an instant, simply
make up the bed in plain white linens and cover it with
a stunning bedspread. Change the cover whenever
you wish for an instant injection of colour and pattern
– eiderdowns, quilts, blankets and throws are just as
versatile, of course. The same applies to your sofa: tuck
a throw, blanket or other length of fabric neatly over it –
back, seat, arms or all over – for a fresh (and inexpensive)
new look.

Choosing bed linen

Quality bed linen will not only feel more
comfortable, but will wash well and last for years.

- **Cotton:** Hardwearing, easy to clean and
  breathable, cotton is a popular choice, and pure
  Egyptian cotton is considered the finest. Styles
  include percale, satin, sateen, waffle, jacquard,
  flannel, jersey and corduroy.
- **Artificial fibres:** Fibres like viscose and rayon are
  soft, durable and absorbent, but may shrink when
  washed.
- **Synthetics:** Polyester, acrylic and nylon are
  great for resisting creases, but can make you
  uncomfortably hot.
- **Blends:** These include polycotton, and can offer
  an ideal combination of the qualities of two or
  more fibres.
- **Linen:** Breathable with a cool, crisp touch, linen
  gets softer as it gets older – but it does need a lot
  of ironing.
- **Silk:** Also highly breathable, silk will keep you
  warm in winter and cool in summer; it's even said
  to reduce wrinkles and make your hair glossy. It
  needs gentle handling.

HOW TO ADD A WOODEN
FRAME TO A MIRROR

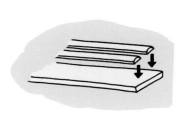 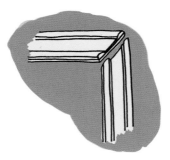 

Measure the length and height of your mirror to determine how large a frame you need. You can use skirting board together with additional moulding for a layered look. You can get the wood cut to size at the DIY shop. Measure the wood that you want to be your outer piece and mark the measurement on the outer edge.

Working inwards from the mark on the outer edge of the wood, cut the wood at a 45° angle; at the opposite end make the 45° cut going in the other direction so the pieces fit together neatly. Continue measuring and cutting all four sides. Sand the wood and then use wood glue to attach the pieces together.

Prime and paint the frame and, when dry, arrange the frame to mount onto your mirror. Glue the middle of the back of each strip of moulding and attach to the mirror. Fill any gaps with paintable caulk and when dry, paint to match.

DISPLAYS

*Make the most of your prized possessions by creating
beautiful, eye-catching displays.*

DISPLAYS ON WALLS

A wall is the ideal blank canvas for a display of almost
any type. Paintings, collages, drawings, photographs and
other flat works of art are the obvious choice – there are
so many possibilities that it's easy to cater for any taste
and style of interior. Surprisingly, single pictures can be
the hardest to hang. Look for convenient alcoves or small
walls, as they tend to get lost on their own on a large wall.
Pairs of pictures often make more visual sense, while a
group of four (two-up, two-down) is smart and sassy.

But why stop at pictures? Textile wall hangings create
just as impressive an effect, whether they be gorgeous
silk robes, wool tapestries, woven rugs or a good-looking
scarf, shawl or banner. And for a really bold display, you
can't beat a wall-mounted three-dimensional object.
Something as simple as a line of vintage plates can be
really decorative, while hanging up your collection of
baskets, handbags, shoe lasts, hats, toy cars and so on
is a great way to store them and show them off at the
same time.

HOW TO ARRANGE A GROUP OF PICTURES

Pictures that are all the same size and identically framed
look amazing hung in regular rows. But it's harder to hang
less co-ordinated pictures. A good method is to lay them
out on the floor, with the largest picture near the centre,
then stand on a chair to look down and get a sense of
how the grouping works. Rearrange as necessary, taking
out any pictures that jar. You may also find that some
need reframing to work in the group. Avoid hanging
pictures in ascending or descending sizes.

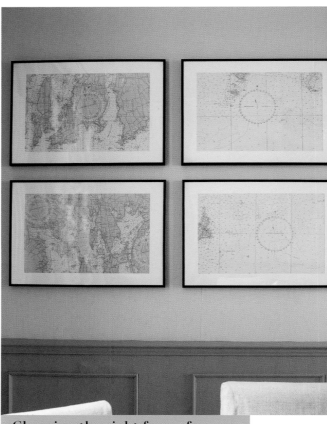

*These framed maps
displayed as a group of
four make a smart and
effective display.*

Choosing the right frame for your picture

A mount, cut at an angle to lead the eye into the
picture, looks professional and can bring out key
colours (though if in doubt, choose off-white). As for
frames, choose a style that is in proportion to your
picture and complements it without dominating.
In general, black, white and silver frames work well
with monochrome or muted pictures, and pale
frames work best with pale pictures. Dark frames can
enhance brightly coloured artwork.

HOW TO HANG A PICTURE

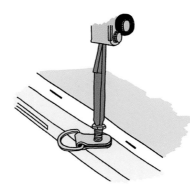

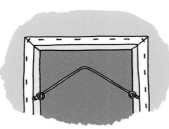

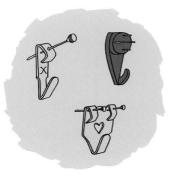

Prepare your picture by making two small holes in the back of the frame at each side, about a third of the way down. Attach screw eyes or D-rings.

Stretch a length of cord, twine or picture wire between the fastenings. The latter is best for heavy pictures as it won't stretch or fray. Knot it securely, allowing a little slack, but not so much that the cord shows above the picture when hung.

What's your wall made from? You can easily bang a nail into timber, and sometimes a picture hook or multiple-pin hook will work on other types of wall, provided the picture is pretty light.

For heavy pictures that you want to hang on a stone, brick, plasterboard or breezeblock wall, you will need to drill a hole and use a suitable wall plug with a screw. Check the wall for hidden pipes or cables before you drill or hammer.

As a general rule, centre a single picture above a sofa, fireplace or table, or within the wall space. Hang with its horizontal centre at eye level (about 145cm/57in is usually recommended) – unless you feel it looks better another way. This is not an exact science, after all.

DISPLAYS IN SHELVES, ALCOVES AND CABINETS

The simplest, most obvious and often most effective way to create a display is by placing objects on a shelf, table, mantelpiece or windowsill, in an alcove or within a cabinet, niche or cubbyhole. Poised and deliberate or delightfully informal, these displays are versatile, space-saving and usually easy to arrange.

What are your options? Well, almost anything can be displayed in this way, from cut-glass perfume bottles to books to pebbles from the beach. Fragile or valuable items are best kept up high or behind glazed doors, of course, and you should avoid putting objects where they will simply become an obstruction (interfering with a blind or taking up space on a coffee table, for example). Consider where they will be in relation to eye level, and ensure that the most interesting features of your display will definitely be visible. Beyond that, enjoy arranging and re-arranging your objects until they suit your style and enhance your space.

THE ART OF DISPLAY

▶ Small objects need to be 'framed' in their surroundings or they will get lost. Large objects can dominate, and need space to breathe. Ensure your displays are proportionate to the space they're in.

▶ Try placing a mirror behind a three-dimensional object on a

Grouping items in different ways on shelves adds variety to a display.

Colourful displays can add interest to simple kitchen schemes.

shelf, so you can see its back, too.

- ▶ Pairs of items are visually very strong. Place them evenly and symmetrically for maximum impact.
- ▶ When displaying groups, an uneven number of items is usually more visually appealing.
- ▶ What shape does your display make? Stand back, squint, and try to see an overall outline, rather than lots of individual objects.
- ▶ Link groups of objects in a display by shape, size, colour and/or texture. Otherwise they can look incoherent.
- ▶ Striking ways to display objects include under Victorian glass domes, in printers' trays, test tubes or flower pots, hung from pegs or over a small ladder, up stairs or thrown over a bust or mannequin. Get creative and express yourself.
- ▶ Lighting will always enhance a display, whether it's natural light falling through a window, a specially fitted spotlight or a table lamp placed nearby.

Displaying objects in glass domes is a way to unify groups of very different items.

FINISHING TOUCHES

When the structural work is done, your walls are finished, your floors are down and the major pieces of furniture are in the right place, it's time to add the details that show off your personality and flair.

Thoughtful final touches add an extra decorative element that really demonstrates who you are. What's more, they are not terribly expensive and can be changed quickly and easily – perhaps with the seasons, or just when you feel like a new look. A few bits and pieces will do the trick. A throw over the arm of a sofa or the back of an armchair is wonderfully appealing, for example, and brings character to even the most boring piece of upholstery. A scattering of cushions – be they square, round, rectangular, bolster-shaped, and featuring piping, buttons or pom-pom trims – has the same effect. A group of vases on a shelf; a row of candles on a mantelpiece; a wicker basket or a coloured plastic tub; a characterful lamp, a carved wooden bowl, a ceramic pot, a pretty mirror – it's not hard to see how all sorts of gorgeous accessories, thoughtfully put together, can be the making of a most attractive and interesting room.

Clean, white surfaces can be embellished without clutter using glassware and tall, delicate plants.

UPCYCLED FURNITURE
AND ACCESSORIES

Turning unloved items of furniture into gorgeous objects of desire
is not as challenging as it might sound.

A coat of paint or a new cover will transform many an ugly duckling, and you can even paste wallpaper (or other attractive paper, such as old maps or sheet music) onto the flat panels of furniture to co-ordinate with your new paint job. Alternatively, use mirror or mosaic tiles to cover a boring surface – such as a clean-lined, pine side table. Another simple trick is to change old knobs or handles. Just unscrew the old ones, fill holes as necessary, and attach your lovely new ones.

If you can use a pair of scissors you can cut out and use a piece of sticky-back plastic (now available in plenty of highly desirable patterns) to line a dull chest or wardrobe.

The result is not only a smooth, clean surface for your clothes, but also a jolt of visual appeal every time you open the door or drawer. And if you can handle a saw, drill and screwdriver there are all sorts of possibilities, from apple-crate shelving to wheeled-pallet coffee tables. It's all about ingenuity and the willingness to have a go.

One last word: leave anything rare, valuable or antique to the experts and, even then, it's best to stick to essential repairs only.

INDEX

DIRECTORY

DIY

B&Q
Everything for DIY.
0845 609 6688
www.diy.com

Brewers
A wide range of decorating materials.
0845 504 5040
www.brewers.co.uk for branches

Buildbase
Builders merchants.
www.buildbase.co.uk for branches

Hobbycraft
The UK's leading art and craft retailer.
0330 026 1400
www.hobbycraft.co.uk

Homebase
Decorating and DIY.
0845 077 8888
www.homebase.co.uk

Jewson
Sustainable timber and building materials.
www.jewson.co.uk for branches

Screwfix
Trade tools, plumbing, electrical, bathrooms and kitchens.
0500 414141
www.screwfix.com

Wickes
Value-for-money home improvement and the building trade.
0370 218 6327
www.wickes.co.uk

Paint

Crown
One of the UK's largest paint manufacturers.
www.crownpaints.co.uk

Dulux
Huge range of household paints.
www.dulux.co.uk

Earthborn
Stylish, high-performance paints that are safer to use and sound for the environment.
01928 734171 for stockists
www.earthbornpaints.co.uk

Farrow & Ball
Unrivalled paint colours made using the finest ingredients and age-old methods.
01202 876141
www.farrow-ball.com

Little Greene
Quality paints with great depth of colour and coverage.
0845 880 5855
www.littlegreene.com

One-stop shops

Argos
Huge range of value furnishings, homeware and accessories.
0845 640 3030
www.argos.co.uk for branches

BHS
Fashionable looks for your home.
www.bhs.co.uk for branches

Cargo
Great value, stylish homewares and furnishings.
0844 848 3300
www.cargohomeshop.com

The Conran Shop
Beautifully designed furniture, lighting, accessories and gifts.
0844 848 4000 for branches
www.conran.com

Debenhams
Department store with a strong range of designer brands.
08445 616161 for branches
www.debenhams.com

Dunelm Mill
Leading home furnishing retailer.
0845 1656565
www.dunelm-mill.com

HomeSense
Designer homewares at up to 60% off.
01923 473 000 for branches
www.homesense.com

House of Fraser
Leading department store.
0845 602 1073
www.houseoffraser.co.uk

Ikea
Affordable solutions for better living.
www.ikea.com for worldwide stores

John Lewis
Everything for the home; never knowingly undersold.
08456 049 049
www.johnlewis.com

Laura Ashley
Much-loved traditional home furnishings.
0871 983 5999
www.lauraashley.com

Marks & Spencer
0845 302 1234
Leading British retailer.
www.marksandspencer.com

Muji
'No brand' quality furniture and accessories.
www.muji.eu for branches

Next
Homewares with style, quality and value for money.
0844 844 8939
www.next.co.uk

Sainsbury's
Homewares and accessories from a leading supermarket.
www.sainsburys.co.uk for branches

Selfridges
Stylish department store with great homewares.
0800 123 400 for branches
www.selfridges.com

Tesco Direct
Huge supermarket with a wide range of products.

0800 323 4050
www.tesco.com/direct

Very
Digital department store.
08448 222 321
www.very.co.uk

World Stores
Everything for the home and garden, online.
0844 931 1005
www.worldstores.co.uk

Decorating

Abode Interiors
Designer furniture and glass coffee tables.
0116 2600 252
www.abode-interiors.co.uk

Abigail Ahern
Quirky, cool statement pieces.
020 7354 8181
www.abigailahern.com

Bathstore
Stylish bathroom products at a good price.
www.bathstore.com for branches

Bombay Duck
Discovering the fabulous in the everyday.
020 8749 3000
www.bombayduck.co.uk

Brume
Made-to-measure window film.
01364 73090
www.brume.co.uk

Carpetright
Contemporary and traditional flooring.
0845 604 5593
www.carpetright.co.uk

Cath Kidston
Witty, reworked English country-house style.
08450 262 440 for branches
www.cathkidston.co.uk

The Contemporary Home
Eclectic interiors products.
02392 469400
www.tch.net

Cox & Cox
Unusual, beautiful and practical products by mail order.
0844 858 0734
www.coxandcox.co.uk

The Curtain Factory Outlet
Curtaining and upholstery fabrics, ready-made curtains and accessories.
020 8492 0093
www.curtainfactoryoutlet.co.uk

Designers Guild
Creative, colourful furnishing fabrics, wallcoverings, upholstery and bed and bath collections.
www.designersguild.com for branches

Etsy
Worldwide marketplace for handmade and unique goods.
www.etsy.com

Fired Earth
An exclusive collection of wall tiles, floor tiles, designer paints, kitchens and bathrooms.
0845 293 8798
www.firedearth.com

Flooring Supplies
The UK's largest online flooring company.
0800 999 8100
www.flooringsupplies.co.uk

Graham & Green
Global, glamorous and gorgeous furniture, lighting and accessories.
020 7243 8908/020 7586 2960
www.grahamandgreen.co.uk

Greengate
Nostalgic and pretty patterned homeware.
www.int.greengate.dk for stores

Habitat
Affordable, functional modern design.
www.habitat.net for stores

Harlequin
Classic-meets-contemporary prints, weaves and

wallcoverings.
www.harlequin.uk.com

Ian Mankin
Natural and organic fabrics, woven in the UK.
020 7722 0997
www.ianmankin.co.uk

Labour & Wait
Timeless, functional products for everyday life.
020 7729 6253
www.labourandwait.co.uk

Liberty
Quintessential English emporium.
020 7734 1234
www.liberty.co.uk

Melin Tregwynt
Traditional Welsh weaving combined with innovative, modern design.
01348 891288/02920 224997
www.melintregwynt.co.uk

Not On The High Street
Original items from creative small businesses.
0845 259 1359
www.notonthehighstreet.com

Online Carpets
Inexpensive carpets and vinyl flooring.
0800 9705 705
www.onlinecarpets.co.uk

Roger Oates
Classic wool flatweave rugs and runners.
01531 632718 for stockists
www.rogeroates.com

Sanderson
Quintessentially English fabrics and wallpapers, bed linen, paint and tableware collections.
www.sanderson-uk.com

Scion
Refreshing new British furnishings brand.
www.scion.uk.com

Sofa.com
Comfy, quality sofas, armchairs and beds.
0845 400 2222
www.sofa.com

SofaSofa
Quality sofas direct from the manufacturers.
01495 244226
www.sofasofa.co.uk

Solid Surface Kitchens Direct
Ready-made worksurfaces, kitchens and kitchen accessories from industry leaders at some of the cheapest prices available.
0845 269 7517
www.solidsurfacekitchens.co.uk/

Store
One-stop shop for your storage needs.
0844 414 2885
www.aplaceforeverything.co.uk

Toast
Laid-back linens, crockery and accessories.
0844 557 0460 for branches
www.toast.co.uk

Topps Tiles
The UK's biggest tile and wood flooring specialist.
0800 783 6262
www.toppstiles.co.uk

Wallpaper Direct
Enormous choice of wallpapers.
01323 430886
www.wallpaperdirect.com

The White Company
Stylish, affordable, designer-quality linens and accessories.
0845 678 8150 for branches
www.thewhitecompany.com

Worktop Express
Leading online solid wood worktop specialist.
0845 2222644
www.worktop-express.co.uk

Zazous
An online shop with original, design-led items.
01843 602800
www.zazous.co.uk

Second-hand, recycled & vintage

After Noah
Unusual and interesting antiques, vintage and contemporary furnishings.
020 7359 4281
www.afternoah.com

Baileys
A mix of vintage and new that's integral to a repair, re-use and rethink philosophy.
01989 561931
www.baileys.com

Bubbledrum
Vintage industrial, reclaimed and handmade items.
020 3092 8974
www.bubbledrum.co.uk

LASSCO
Prime resource for architectural antiques, salvage and curiosities.
020 7749 9944
www.lassco.co.uk

Masco Salvage
Reclaimed architectural features and traditional building materials.
01285 760886
www.mascosalvage.com

Re
A fab mix of pieces that are rare, remarkable, recycled and restored.
01434 634567
www.re-foundobjects.com

Retropolitan
Stylish and affordable decorative vintage homeware.
07870 422182
www.retropolitan.co.uk

Salvo
Gateway to the world of architectural salvage and antiques.
www.salvoweb.com

Winter's Moon
A quirky assortment of vintage, recycled or handmade furniture and home accessories.
07783 768503
www.wintersmoon.co.uk

PUBLISHER'S ACKNOWLEDGEMENTS

TEXT
Katherine Sorrell and Nina Sharman

COMMISSIONED PHOTOGRAPHY
Heather Hobhouse: 12–13, 18, 19TR, 22, 24TR, 25ML, 30, 31, 33BL, 42, 44, 45 51TI, 51TR, 51ML, 70, 90, 92, 97TL, 98, 99TL, 112, 113, 118, 119, 120, 124, 127TR, 128BL, 130, 138, 139, 143, 145B, 146T, 152, 158, 161BR, 162T, 164TR, 165, 169T, 170, 171BL, 172, 173, 175, 176, 177, 180, 181, 184BR, 188, 189, 207B, 216T, 217, 219BL.
Holly Jolliffe: cover photography, 2, 4, 6–7, 14, 19BL, 20–21, 24BR, 25MT, 25BR, 26, 27, 28, 29, 32, 33TR, 34, 35, 38, 40, 48, 49, 50, 51MR, 51BL, 51BR, 59, 61, 62, 64, 66, 73, 76, 77, 78, 79, 80, 82, 84, 86, 88, 96, 97TR, 99TR, 102, 104, 106, 111, 114, 115, 116–117, 122, 123, 125, 126, 127BL, 128TR, 131, 132, 133, 134, 135, 136, 137, 142, 144, 145T, 146BL, 146–147, 148, 150, 156, 160, 161TL, 162BR, 163, 164BL, 168, 169BL, 171TR, 174, 178, 179, 204, 205, 205TL, 208, 209, 210, 211, 212, 213, 214, 216B, 218, 219TR.
Styling: Emily Blunden.

ILLUSTRATIONS
Zoe More O'Ferrall: cover illustrations, 15, 16–17, 37, 43, 47, 60, 63, 65, 71, 72, 79, 81, 83, 101, 103, 121, 149, 213, 215.
Julia Rothman: 23, 41, 53, 55, 57, 75, 107, 108, 109.

The publishers would like to thank the following individuals, companies and organisations for supplying images: Alexander & Pearl 93BML; Alison at Home 93ML; Laura Ashley 91TR; Avenue Floors 39TMR; Bathstore 56, 100, 190, 191, 192T, 193, 195BL, 196, 197, 200, 201, 202, 203; Crucial Trading 39TL, 39TML, 93CML; Dupont™ Corian© 58CM, 153CMR; EasiPanel 58BM; Fabrics & Papers 58TM, 91TL, 91MR; Fired Earth 39CMR, 39MR, 39BML, 93TMR; Formica 153CML; Forbo 39TR; Granorte 39BR, 58TR, 58ML, 93TML; Ikea 129, 140, 141, 151, 153MR, 153, 155, 157, 159, 166, 167, 182, 183, 184TR, 185, 186–187, 192B, 194, 195TR, 198, 199; Kahrs 39ML; John Lewis 93CMR, 93MR, 93BR; Loaf 93TR; Ian Mankin 91TML, 91ML, 91CML, 91MR, 93TL; Okite 153TML; Quick-step 39CML; Red Candy 93BMR; The Rubber Floor Store 39BMR; Sanderson 91TMR, 91BL, 91BML, 91BMR, ; SCIN Gallery 153BL; Scion 91BR; Second Nature 153TL, 153TML, 153TR, 153BML; Sofa. com 93BL; SurfaceForm 58BL; Tile Mountain 58MR; UK Flooring Direct 39BL; White & Reid 153ML.

We apologise in advance for any unintentional omission or neglect and will be pleased to insert the appropriate acknowledgement for any individuals, companies or organisations in any subsequent edition of this work.

STUDIO LAMBERT
Tim Harcourt, Creative Director
Tom Garland, Executive Producer
Chi Ukairo, Series Producer
Lindsay Bradbury, Commissioning Editor for BBC
Matt Werendel, Production Manager
Nina Haines, Production Executive
Jo Crawley, Head of Production
Martin Connery, Producer Director
Nicky Hammond, Producer Director
Edward Robinson, Design Producer
Lucy Welch, Design Producer
Hannah Moorman, Associate Producer
Kate McPhee, Associate Producer
Zoë Millard, DV Director
Rebecca Morris, DV Director
Charlie Slade, DV Director
Emily Hudson, Casting Executive
Jane Tweddle, Casting Producer
Olivia Thompson, Casting Assistant Producer
James Alexander, Casting Researcher
Holly Newman, Casting Researcher
Eleanor Priestman, Casting Researcher
James Phillips, History Researcher
Tim Appleford, Junior Researcher
Susanna Hudson, Junior Researcher
Claire Ennion, Location Coordinator
Karen Woodman, Production Coordinator
Matt Cotton, Production Secretary
Alasdair Colquhoun, Runner
Faye Denfhy, Runner
Chris Keenan, Director of Photography
Bala Bailey, Camera Operator
Mark Sowden, Sound Operator
Matt Turner, Sound Operator
Dickie Ashenden, Construction Team
Jayson Dillimore, Construction Team
Wayne Perrey, Construction Team
Stuart Plant, Construction Team
Jo Pollock, Construction Team
Dean Taylor, Construction Team
Kim Teasdale, Construction Team
Jonathan Towers, Construction Team
Steve Wilson, Construction Team

First published in the United Kingdom in 2015 by
Pavilion
1 Gower Street
London
WC1E 6HD

ISBN 978-1-90981-586-5

A CIP catalogue record for this book is available from the British Library.

10 9 8 7 6 5 4 3 2 1

Reproduction by Rival Colour Ltd, UK
Printed and bound by L.E.G.O. SpA, Italy

This book can be ordered direct from the publisher at
www.pavilionbooks.com